NEVER ENOUGH

US Festival, California, September 1982
(Stanley Greene/NOOR)

Never Enough

A Way Through Addiction

Barney Hoskyns

Constable • London

CONSTABLE

First published in Great Britain in 2017 by Constable

1 3 5 7 9 10 8 6 4 2

A CIP catalogue record for this book
is available from the British Library.

ISBN: 978-1-47212-553-8 (hardback)
ISBN: 978-1-47212-552-1 (trade paperback)

Typeset in Sabon by SX Composing DTP, Rayleigh, Essex
Printed and bound in Great Britain by Clays Ltd, St Ives plc

Papers used by Constable are from well-managed forests
and other responsible sources.

MIX
Paper from
responsible sources
FSC® C104740

Constable
An imprint of
Little, Brown Book Group
Carmelite House
50 Victoria Embankment
London EC4Y 0DZ

An Hachette UK Company
www.hachette.co.uk

www.littlebrown.co.uk

For Christian Preston

Contents

In those moments of silence with Antony – in that instant of 'Could we actually do this?' – I know I am standing at the edge of a precipice. I know that this can only be the wrong thing to do. But then, as if trading in my soul, I go for it. I tell Antony I want him to inject me. I am crossing over to some other side. I am joining the tribe of the scarred and damned.

Or do I simply think what all prospective users think? I'll just try it; I won't do it again; it's not as if one shot will get me hopelessly hooked.

But one shot will get me hopelessly hooked. One shot will be too many and – as I will hear repeatedly in years to come – a thousand never enough.

PART 1
MY CHEMICAL ROMANCE

'It is not to the people to whom they bring the pleasure of sleep or a genuine well-being that these drugs are an absolute necessity; it is not by such people as these that they would be bought at any price, bartered against all the sick man's possessions, but by that other class of sick men . . . those whom the medicine does not send to sleep, to whom it gives no thrill of pleasure, but who, so long as they are without it, are prey to an agitation which at any price, even the price of their own death, they need desperately to end.'

Marcel Proust, *Time Regained* (translated by Andreas Mayor and Terence Kilmartin)

'Home is where the needle marks / Try to heal my broken heart . . .'

Gil Scott-Heron, 'Home is Where the Hatred is'

The brilliant Tasmanian grips my hand with surprising force, transporting me back thirty-five years to my early awe at his withering intelligence and prodigious reputation. 'You were always in your rooms shooting up!' he all but yelps. He is clasping my hand hard. 'Adam had to take me to one side and ask me to go easy on you!'

I want to protest, mildly, that I was not shooting up in my rooms, but I suspect that – to the degree that he thinks about this former student at all – I remain fixed in his mind as the emaciated amphetamine user with hennaed hair who, in the summer of 1980, stunned him and others by taking a First Class degree in English Language and Literature.

I am here, on an October evening in a tall house in Vauxhall, to pay homage to a man who radically reshaped the way I looked at literature. Generations of Peter Conrad's former students from four decades – theatre critics, right-wing columnists, others of a doomed breed of media professional – have come along to confess that they too were disciples of the author of *Shandyism* and *Imagining America*. Since, for most of those Oxford years, I felt on the outside of most things, it's unexpectedly moving to stand here and learn that others felt the same way about him.

'We are all the children of Peter,' announces one of the organizers of the evening – and of a sort of *festschrift* in Peter's honour. 'Which does not mean we expect presents at Christmas.'

At the night's winding-down, after he's been presented with the bound collection of essays and poems and thanked us with an unscripted speech that proves his mischievous wit undimmed, I approach Peter to say goodbye. Once more he takes my hand and holds it hard; I feel a warmth I never knew was there in all the time he taught me. I don't suppose I even *shook* his hand in three years.

'I have to tell you that, of all the people here, you're the one I'd have *least* recognized,' he says to me. 'Not because you look so different – now that I see you – but because you've become a man. And you were such a boy.'

I tell him I *was* a boy, little more than a child. I say I was hopelessly lost and unsure. 'I didn't have the first idea who I was. But I want you to know how proud I am to have been taught by you.'

As I stride back up the long straight road towards the river and the railway, I'm aware of emotions I hadn't expected to feel. Grateful to Peter for noticing that, at fifty-two, I am now a man. Pleased to have known this maverick Antipodean who tilted literature on its axis for me. But also deeply sad for the boy he knew those decades ago, about to be left behind by his graduating contemporaries. I grieve for that boy and wonder how he made it through alive. If I could, I would go back and make it all right for him.

A week after learning I had got my First, I sat in a basement flat on the west side of Clapham Common and asked my best friend to inject me with heroin.

To this day I don't quite know why.

● ● ●

The very word was enough to strike dread into me as a child. Like 'cancer', 'heroin' seemed synonymous with death. If you took it you would die, for junkies were the walking dead. There were many stupidly dangerous things you might do in your life, but shooting heroin would not be one of them.

Slowly the idea of heroin – and of syringes – changes as you move through adolescence. Not that it becomes exactly alluring, but it begins to beguile. You can be doing other, 'softer' drugs, yet you are aware that 'King Heroin' – as James Brown personified it – is the preserve of the damned and formerly beautiful, a diabolical deal on which you cannot renege. And if you are becoming progressively unhappier in that adolescence, if you're not making that journey in the way the majority of people do, you too can be seduced by the vision of those who've gone over to the other side with the emperor of analgesic narcotics.

For me it wasn't Charlie Parker or Keith Richards: it was, of all the musical stars, Diana Ross who first graphically showed what heroin addiction involved; who, tying a red rubber tube around her skinny Supremes arm in *Lady Sings the Blues*, displayed the sweet oblivion that smack promised. Not that you have the first notion, until you experience it, of what that oblivion feels like; of how profoundly it removes you from the world, from caring at all. Before you use it, all you know is what heroin looks like from the outside, how it shields the user behind an impenetrable barrier of Cool.

(Moviestore/REX/Shutterstock)

My Chemical Romance

It's too easy to look back now and say: what a cliché to believe that Keith and Lou and Iggy and Johnny Thunders were so hip in their black clothes and black sunglasses; to have subscribed to the doctrine of 'Wasted Elegance' as we absorbed it from the pages of the *New Musical Express*. (If the phrase wasn't coined by the *NME*'s Nick Kent – that second-string icon of opiated enervation – it should have been.) But if the Keith Richards of the Rolling Stones' most satanically majestic period (1968–1972, why bother arguing) wasn't cool, what *is*?

If it had only been the dark lords of rock, with their riffs of love and death, the spell might have worn off. It was only later we learned that Lou Reed, author of the greatest heroin song of all (the one with the brilliantly bald title 'Heroin'), was more devoted to amphetamine and alcohol than to smack. But junkie cool was brought altogether closer to home by the presence of my very own proxy rock star at Westminster School.

Two years older and a Queen's Scholar to boot, Richard was a walking wet dream for anyone half in love with easeful self-destruction. To say I had a platonic crush on this svelte genius as he hovered across Little Dean's Yard on silver platform boots would badly understate my feelings for him. It was whispered that he was the most brilliant boy who'd ever been at the school: steeped in Greek, fluent in French, often spotted with arcane and possibly occult volumes under his arm. And yet he looked like a glam-rock god in his platforms and his mirrored

Aviator shades – or like the mysterious figure on the cover of his beloved Thomas Pynchon's story 'Mortality and Mercy in Vienna'.

It was only later, at Oxford, that Richard began to henna the dense helmet of dark hair that now makes me think, oddly, of David Miliband. It was certainly at Oxford that I uttered my first trembling words to him and learned he was everything he appeared to be: frighteningly clever, well-versed in the works of the Velvet Underground and the Stooges, and on at least nodding acquaintance with Class A chemicals I hadn't yet sampled.

Ah, Richard, did you really exist or did we have to invent you? You were Rainer Maria Rilke at Villa Nellcôte, you were Lou Reed at the *École Normale Supérieure*. You'd read every book ever written, even studies of astrophysics and morphogenesis that would have stumped your slow-witted admirer. You'd seen every film by Godard and Bresson and Jacques Rivette. Every sentence you spoke in your close-to-camp voice was crystalline in its lucid perfection. Or perhaps you were only playing the polymath for those of us who'd signed up to your cult.

Richard was exotic and magnetic in other ways. He seemed to issue from some mongrel aristocracy: part Australian, part *mittel*-Eurotrash, part Martian, but then again nearly *sui generis*. Westminster was not Eton, but it had its smattering of double-barrelled bluebloods, and Richard had ties to those. He was a missing link between Chatsworth and *Metallic KO*, between Proust and the Baader-Meinhof gang. As I grew more curious about dangerous drugs it became clearer that he knew more than a few of the beautiful and damned offspring of dukes and industrialists.

Heroin lurked in the margins of privileged life in that era. At Oxford I was at a college where Brideshead was revisited almost nightly – delighting my maternal grandfather, who'd been in the Bullingdon in the late twenties – but already there were Old Etonians dabbling in the black arts of blackened spoons. Some even dressed like Johnny Thunders and the Heartbreakers, tousled public schoolboys with Lower East Side track marks on their arms. They wore dirty jackets with thin lapels, bought with trust-fund money on the King's Road, and t-shirts artfully torn and emblazoned with nihilistic scrawls. Some spent half their lives driving too fast between Oxford and London: God forbid there was a party in Chelsea they might miss, even if it meant hurtling back up the M40 at dawn to make a tutorial and thus avoid being – in that most absurdly archaic of Oxbridge phrases – 'sent down'.

The most infamous of all these wayward sons wasn't at Oxford at all. He was the Honourable Charlie Tennant, a gaunt cupid who haunted the back streets of London SW3 and was already dragging a sackful of scary stories behind him. Compared to Charlie, other aristo smackheads were mere amateurs. His rep made him a golem of junk, his close brushes with fatal overdose the stuff of legend. (He did die prematurely, but of AIDS.)

The closest I got to Charlie was a photograph in an album of holiday snaps belonging to a friend who fronted a public-school 'punk' band that emulated the fey, heroin-infused Only Ones. Years later I visited the latter group's frontman, Peter Perrett, in his huge decaying home in Forest Hill, though my efforts to help the author of 'Another Girl, Another Planet' – a veritable anthem for posh junkies in 1978 – were wholly in vain.

These are among the memories that return from a time when I was becoming increasingly unhappy, ever more lacking in confidence, pretending to be cool, and desperate to impress Peter Conrad with abstruse essays on Restoration Comedy or the Victorian novel. 'I always thought it funny,' he once said to me, 'that the only really good essay you wrote was about, of all people, Doctor Johnson.'

• • •

I wouldn't say that in 1974 I had a drug problem, even if I now date my chemical abuse to sly swigs of Bulmers Woodpecker Cider in my parents' shed in Suffolk, where I spent school holidays and *exeat* weekends.

Within weeks of arrival at Westminster in early 1973 I was 'smoking dope', as we all put it back then. Later came speed, acid, and the first expensive snorts of cocaine. Principal partner-in-crime was Antony, who should by rights have been at Eton but instead stuck out as unabashedly aristocratic in Westminster's sea of pseudo-meritocracy.

At Westminster you kept schtum about privilege and large allowances. Not Antony, whose privileged upbringing turned out to be unhappier than any of us could have imagined. I led a kind of double life, going to concerts and smoking dope with boys from Clapham and Kentish Town; then going to Kensington and smoking *lots* of dope with Antony, who was defiantly self-destructive *and* cleverer than anyone else in my year.

I was told that Westminster had been a hotbed of narcotic vice before my arrival at the school. If the new headmaster, handsome and silver-haired as an American president, had purged the worst offenders, mood-altering smokables remained rife in the shadows of the abbey. Sixth-formers tottered about Little Dean's Yard in greatcoats, clutching double-albums under their arms.

In my year, Alex rolled the best and biggest joints, but Mike smoked more of them than anyone else and was expelled from Westminster as a consequence. We *all* smoked cigarettes, piling into Gino's coffee bar at break time for Benson & Hedges and watery cappuccinos, piling back into class like a single giant ashtray on multiple pairs of legs. No teacher ever so much as remarked on the unholy stench.

Those of my friends who'd had elder brothers at the school acted as conduits of the drug subculture, carrying the spirit of the late sixties into the decadent new decade. Free festivals and protest marches already felt like ancient history to us. We young dudes danced not to the Beatles but to the pied pipers of glam: as David Bowie wrote in a timeless song he donated to Mott the Hoople, 'we never got it off on that revolution stuff'.

Yet with Alex and Michael and Christian – all younger brothers of 'Old Wets' – I snapped out of glam and into the stoned order of the Deadheads. I fell in love with mystic bearded groovers: with the Band and Little Feat, with John Martyn and the Led Zeppelin of *Led Zeppelin III*. Fuzzy Sundays unravelled at the Roundhouse, where cheesecloth-garbed pub rockers and *ZigZag*-reading West Coast wannabes played all afternoon but where we never got quite stoned enough not to feel jejune. There were stinky Afghan coats and spooling guitar leads, and the pong of patchouli competed with the smog of Moroccan hash. As Zippy the Pinhead would have asked, 'Are we having fun yet?' I was never quite sure.

To the older heads at the Roundhouse, would I have denied buying those sensational singles by Slade and T. Rex? Would I have concealed the glossy gatefold sleeve of Roxy Music's *For Your Pleasure*? Probably. For I was now a neophyte in some quasi-tribal hangover from psychedelic Americana, schlepping up to Cheapo Cheapo in Soho every Wednesday in search of second-hand albums by Quicksilver Messenger Service and the New Riders of the Purple Sage.

THE AMAZING ZIGZAG CONCERT
ROUNDHOUSE CHALK FARM **N.W.1.**
MICHAEL NESMITH
RED RHODES
(ONLY U.K. APPEARANCE)
JOHN STEWART
HELP YOURSELF
CHILLI WILLI
AND THE RED HOT PEPPERS
STARRY EYED AND LAUGHING
SUN. 28TH **APRIL 1974**

The real truth was that I never even liked dope, pot, weed, grass, Afghan Black, Moroccan Red. I'm not convinced that my friends did either, though we all put on brave faces as we claimed to be having high times. Low-grade paranoia and disorientation were not things I'd ever have become addicted to, and yet I smoked yards of this stuff with my buddies, sitting for hours in the attics of their parents' homes in Camden and Hampstead. At least the interminable extemporizations of the Grateful Dead and their ilk made sense under the influence of these herbs.

13

Though my own parents would have been alarmed had they known what I was up to, I don't look back at the mid-seventies and see my subsequent problems as inevitable. For all those of us who graduated to 'harder' drugs, as many moved away from them entirely. It's too obvious to point out that the predisposition to addiction comes not in packets but in people.

Antony did not listen to the Grateful Dead. He did not accompany Alex and Michael and Shane and me to the Roundhouse or the Rainbow. He did not see the Who-headlined Charlton show of 1974, or attend the Knebworth Festivals of 1975 and 1976 with me and Tom. He didn't even see the Rolling Stones at Earl's Court, though he later became a pal of Mick Jagger's. Nor did he sit around with Tim and me as I embarked on my new discovery of soul music, listening to records by Rufus and Bill Withers or immersing myself in the back catalogues of Stax and Motown.

Certainly Antony did not make the faintest concession to sartorial norms of the period, preferring to dress in Jermyn Street suits and shirts that provided the perfect disguise for his narcotic activities. If Henry James had written a heroin addict into *The Portrait of a Lady*, Antony would have been that addict; he even had an American heiress for a mother.

What Antony really loved to do was smoke a lot of dope – and, later on, drop acid – before meeting for tea at, say, Fortnum & Mason. Mixing these two worlds was to him a splendid game, especially when he had a small audience to entertain. Often that was just me – the I to his Withnail, the Lenù to his Lila, the indigent Ryder to his trust-funded Flyte (had Waugh's feckless scion been a good deal cleverer) – shaking with laughter over Earl Grey and sandwiches as he ran through his repertoire of impersonations, usually of teachers I could never have speared with such lancing precision.

'Had lunch with A. in some psychedelic pizza place,' I scrawled in a Letts pocket diary in the baking heat of July 1976. 'We talked rubbish in an incorrigibly self-satisfied way. He is good company though fey, fastidious, indolent, intolerant, conceited, cold-hearted . . .'

Sometimes as I sat with Antony, hypnotized by his pitiless Jack Nicholson eyes, I wondered what Alex or Mat or Shane or Tim would have thought had they strolled at that instant into the Fortnum's tearooms. No less than my parents, they regarded Antony as a malign influence: spoiled, decadent, snobbish. Was I then myself snobbish by association, or at least aspirant? In hindsight I oscillated in almost bipolar fashion between an envy of Antony and an innate Roundhead scorn for all things Cavalier.

Some saw Antony as the archetype of the Poor Little Rich Boy, his wealth an ineffective substitute for the love he'd never had as a boy. Yet his chaos rarely manifested externally; from the outside he was as rigidly controlled as William S. Burroughs. I know now that he was actively seeking oblivion in ways I was not. He carried an agonizing wound I could not have inferred and only grasped when, years later, he confessed it to me. As long as he could keep me – and others – in stitches, he could stand to be in his own skin.

• • •

It was with Antony, in 1977, that I flew for the first time to America: specifically to the Manhattan that had obsessed me since 1969, when my father returned from a business trip with the gifts of a small plastic Empire State Building and a guidebook filled with technicolour views of New York City.

My Manhattan fantasies were analogous to the Romantics' notions of the Sublime: not for nothing had André Kertész christened one of his famous Gotham photographs 'Wall Street Canyon'. I was enraptured by the Mammon that the city represented. It was a metropolis above and beyond all others, a nexus of glamour and squalor, a place I had by now seen many times in films and absorbed from punk and disco and older doo-wop records.

It was also already a place defined by drugs. Abetted by Warhol and his acolytes, Lou Reed had immortalized the figure of the White Boy Copping In Harlem, but a subsequent generation of nihilists had made heroin integral to the city's underground art. If Tom Wolfe had been correct in saying that a doorman in New York City was not simply a doorman but a *New York City* doorman, then a New York junkie was never just a junkie. As on the cover of Steely Dan's 1976 album *The Royal Scam*, Mammon's towers glared monstrously down at the street creatures scuttling in its gutters, but every New Yorker was tall simply by association with the scale of the place.

The first time I was in New York alone, I felt so scared that I adopted a phony streetwise accent for the benefit of the taxi driver outside the Port Authority Bus Terminal: 'Empire Hotel,' I declared, 'on sixty-thoid 'n' Broadway . . .' I had put myself so far inside Travis Bickle's head that the menacing swell of Bernard Herrmann's music was spreading through my brain.

Antony and I arrived, apocalyptically, on the afternoon of 13 July, the date of an infamous New York blackout. (I later learned that Johnny Thunders had flown back from London on the very same day. Also arriving at JFK was Carlos Alberto, the Brazilian football legend who'd just signed for the New York Cosmos.) Sadly we were not in the city to witness it; instead we awoke in the morning on the north shore of Long Island, greeted by pictures of mass lootings in the *New York Times*.

Though we spent only one night in Manhattan, the experience of being there in the blanketing humidity of a siren-strafed midsummer night – of taking a cab uptown to eat at fabled Elaine's and then ascending the Empire State – consummated my love for the streets and 'scrapers I'd seen in *Kojak*, *Breakfast at Tiffany's*, *The Apartment*, *Rosemary's Baby*, *Trash*, *Panic in Needle Park* and *The French Connection*; that I'd heard in *The Velvet Underground and Nico* and *The New York Dolls*, *Horses* and *The Ramones*.

When I arrived at Oxford that autumn I came with an armful of albums that spoke to me of Gotham: *The Ramones*, *Talking Heads: 77* and Television's *Marquee Moon* were the three I treasured most. 'Broadway looked so medieval, it seemed to flap like little pages,' Television's Tom Verlaine sang nonsensically and almost psychedelically; 'I fell sideways laughing with a friend from many stages . . .' It might have been Antony and me as we'd wandered sleazy 42nd Street in search of a porn movie, settling eventually on *Peach Fuzz*. To those albums I would soon add Odyssey's 'Native New Yorker', a twelve-inch disco masterwork arranged by Charlie Calello, the genius who'd orchestrated albums by Laura Nyro.

New York for me had become a place of febrile intellect and slumming debauchery, and I thought of little else but getting back there as quickly as possible. (I have done so, at least once every subsequent year of my life.) A compilation album appeared with a cover that turned the Empire State Building into a giant hypodermic. Hopheads in Harlem, like strung-out tenor men on 52nd Street, must have experienced the same hallucination ever since the building was completed in 1931.

Other records cemented the bond between New York music and dangerous narcotics. The first album by Suicide, whose cheap synthesizer sequencing was an inspired mimesis of urban dehumanization, was seldom off the turntable in the room that Adam and Tim shared at Christ Church. Nor can I forget the Heartbreakers' 'Chinese Rocks', an anthem of heroin enslavement penned one productive afternoon by Douglas 'Dee Dee Ramone' Colvin (with minor subsequent assistance from Richard 'Hell' Meyers). Long before I ever did smack, these records permitted a vicarious affair with hard drugs. Not that I ever mentioned this to Adam or Tim or to David. I don't believe I even discussed heroin with Richard, to whom I'd finally been introduced by Adam.

What any of this had to do with dissecting *The Owl and the Nightingale* or Robert Browning's 'My Last Duchess' I cannot really say. I longed to be good at English – which really I was not – but once I'd climbed the ancient stairwell to my rooms I dreamed only of being a fucked-up rock star with a drug habit and several pairs of Ray-Bans. 'You were always in your rooms shooting up!'

I guess I fooled at least one person.

• • •

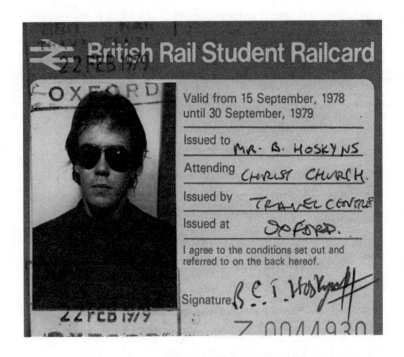

My Chemical Romance

I don't think I knew how lonely I was. I was only just starting to feel painfully different from everyone around me. Certainly it was easier to disappear into fantasies of remote stardom than to engage in real life and relationships. My peers were doing what nineteen-year-old males *should* have been doing: acting, writing for *Isis*, taking girls out. Too often I was to be found – or not even sought out – in my rooms, my nose in *Ulysses* or *Martin Chuzzlewit* but constantly anxious that I was missing the point of them.

I'd had awkward sexual encounters but was secretly afraid of females and what they could reduce me to. I developed a crush on a girl I couldn't bear to approach, preferring to leave notes in her cubbyhole in college. Years later I found myself face to face with this woman in London and felt pitifully grateful to her for not reminding me of my humiliation.

Time crawled by so slowly back then. There was nothing to do in 1978 except feel things – or *not* feel things because I'd long ago split off my feelings in order to bear them. I was an addict waiting to happen but hadn't found the right potion. For all my fascination with it, heroin remained *verboten*, tagged with a death's-head insignia. I drank alcohol but didn't like being drunk; smoked weed but didn't love being stoned.

Periodically Antony – who'd failed on his first attempt to get into Oxford – visited with drugs. Cautious and scared, I embarked on my first acid trips with him. One was hilariously happy, a night of hallucinating playing cards in the ancient walls, giant newspapers unfurling across the pre-dawn sky. Another hollowed me out to a point of pure terror where all was blood and emptiness and the only thing saving me from total madness was listening repeatedly to the Ramones' song 'I'm Affected'. I never did LSD again.

I think I only started to *use* drugs in my final year at Oxford. Amphetamine became an essential aid for revision as I ploughed back through Shakespeare and Yeats and James, surfacing at lunchtime in the reddish hair I'd hennaed in tribute to Richard. One day, I told myself, there will be a life beyond Finals; I'll be able to walk in woods and fields again. But for now I will keep the blinkers on.

An odd thing happened as the exams loomed in that summer of 1980. As I sat studying in the Bodleian Library one morning I impulsively wrote a note to Sara, the prettiest girl in the whole university. I invited her to come to Glyndebourne to see Strauss's *Der Rosenkavalier*, tickets for which my parents had bought me as a twenty-first birthday present. I cannot think where I found the sheer chutzpah to try this on. To my amazed pleasure I got back a flirtatious card of acceptance that instantly made me feel like a god.

Years later I would hear the phrase 'narcissistic elevation' trip from a therapist's tongue. So *that* was all it was, I thought with a wan smile.

• • •

I sit with Antony in the damp Clapham basement. My parents, who live upstairs, are gone. It is a weekday afternoon, grey and forgettable.

It is only recently that I've had confirmed what I'd suspected, which is that Antony has moved beyond dope/pot/weed and LSD into more serious substances. Somehow we get talking about heroin and he says, slyly, 'As it happens I have some on me.' He is twenty years old, eight months my junior. I titter at his sheer naughtiness and we regard each other for a second like criminals hatching some hare-brained heist.

Could we? Dare we?

I am not even aware that I'm fundamentally unhappy enough to risk everything in this one mad moment. Antony was always likely to become a junkie, but I have only ever flirted with addiction, tiptoed on its wild side. Yet I can see – at least in hindsight, all these years later – that the future is upon me and that I have no notion of what I am supposed to do with the life that stretches ahead. Quietly my friends have been growing up and mapping out their futures. Tim is going to intern on Wall Street. David is planting his feet on the academic ladder. Adam is off to Washington to start a postgraduate journalism course. I have simply assumed that something will happen to me and that the way will become clear. But the way is not becoming clear and I am unhappily conscious of being the same manchild I was at thirteen. I hadn't realized that those Careers Advice Officers were serious. I hadn't known that when we were all out in Oxford carousing, I was alone in not grasping that middle-class life would be about salaries and families and mortgages and pension plans. Which is why my closest friend is someone who doesn't want to grow up either. Except that Antony doesn't *need* to grow up. His money means that other people do his growing up *for* him.

My father has made nepotistic gestures, fixing appointments with avuncular publishers and jowly Fleet Street columnists. But these veterans take one look at me and see that I sorely lack drive and discipline – that I have no useful hunger and am profoundly unworldly. I simply wish to be recognized for a talent I do not even believe I possess. How do you get anywhere in this world, and what do you want to do anyway? I want to write but don't know what to write. I think that somehow you can simply be creative and it will translate into sustenance. The painful truth, as anyone looking in from outside might have gauged, is that I have no idea who I am and no honest way of articulating how I feel. I am a mess of postures and attitudes that I attempt to express in a cheap red exercise book:

I cannot step into the world. There is no room for me. I talked to a buffoon at John Murray who – on

*the strength of his being about to publish a novel
by a railway engineer – advised me to become a
delivery boy. If the vegetable-faced ass had not been
a friend of my father's, I would have crammed his
Royal Academy baked potato into his face. If there
is no job, I shall not 'take' a job.*

In those moments of silence with Antony – in that instant
of 'Could we actually do this?' – I know I am standing
at the edge of a precipice. I know that this can only be
the wrong thing to do. But then, as if trading in my soul,
I go for it. I tell Antony I want him to inject me. I am
crossing over to some other side. I am joining the tribe of
the scarred and damned.

Or do I simply think what all prospective users think?
*I'll just try it; I won't do it again; it's not as if one shot
will get me hopelessly hooked.*

But one shot will get me hopelessly hooked. One shot
will be too many and – as I will hear repeatedly in years
to come – a thousand never enough.

I look away as the needle slips into the bulging vein
in the crook of my arm. ('You'll feel a little prick,' I
almost hear Antony whispering. 'It's nothing to worry
about.') A moment of horrified disbelief passes as he
draws my blood back into the barrel of the syringe and
a tiny crimson cloud swirls within the murky brown
liquid. I watch as he pushes the mixture into my bloodstream and am straightaway engulfed by a sensation I

could not possibly have anticipated. I feel as if I've been benignly slugged, yet I remain conscious. The taste in my sinuses is roughly akin to burnt caramel. What is actually happening is that diamorphine is crossing my blood–brain barrier, rapidly deacetylating into inactive 3-monoacetylmorphine and active 6-monoacetylmorphine – and then into the morphine that binds to my μ-opioid receptors and causes a euphoria that is simultaneously analgesic and anxiolytic.

I salute the dope fiend who first applied the word 'fix' to the effect of heroin. For the drug is a one-size-fits-all remedy for the core angst of sentient being, allaying and overriding all uncertainties. It stops the world whirling around you and stops you whirling around *it*. Lou Reed may have tried in 'Heroin' to 'nullify my life' but he was also, brilliantly, trying 'for the kingdom if I can'. No wonder that when Bayer brought diamorphine to market in 1895, the company named it after the Greek *heros*.

Lou's kingdom is that sovereign peace otherwise denied to frightened, fragmented souls. Heroin is a portal to invincibility, shielding you against fear, or at least removing it to a remote location in the way morphine historically displaced the pain of wounded soldiers and cancer patients. I can still see my crippling self-doubt but – most precious of all gifts – I can no longer *feel* it. I am, in the phrase coined by another eloquent dope fiend, 'out of it'.

I rise to my feet with the contagion in me and consciously phrase the thought, 'I want to feel like this always.' My limbs have thirsted for this moment, longed to be made whole. How could you not wish to be in this state, with this force field around you? 'That's the lousy thing about drugs,' Lucia Berlin wrote. 'They work.'

Antony grins at me as the high priest smiles at the novice. Again, neither of us needs to speak: there will be many moments like this. I do not even feel nauseous, as so many do on making their heroin debuts. I am a duck that's taken effortlessly to this water, as if my main handicap in life has long been a deficiency of endorphins.

I have known Antony since we were thirteen and this is the event our adventures have led us to. We are blood brothers via a shared works (the street term I thenceforth employ for a syringe). I am now infected with the same dependency, and soon my life will swing crudely between stonedness and heightened self-loathing. The more I use, the less tolerable I will be to myself without heroin in me.

I've signed up for the ride, and one day I will want to get off it. Which is when the fear will really begin.

• • •

Sara was petite and boyish. She possessed an irresistible face, with sea-green eyes skirted by short dark hair. She smelled of Diorissimo, a scent I would crave as keenly as I craved the scent of heroin cooking in a spoon with lemon juice – or even, eventually, the sulphurous smell of a match struck to heat the underside of a spoon. (To this day I can't light a match without an instant Pavlovian recall of the drug.)

Loving her is the beginning, and everything since the beginning directly involves her. Which is not to say I cannot quickly recreate that perfectly achieved solitude in which the last three years are coated.

Sara did not know who she was and so, like me, affected to be a number of things she was not: composed, enigmatic, at ease with social superiors. She'd broken several hearts by the time she took a chance on me. I was a nobody and she was already a proto-'It' girl in London, operating in spheres of fashion and aspiration that held no allure for me – or that I was ineligible to enter.

Certain almost Jamesian figures are plotting to get her away from me. I am not invited with her. I am not a stylish enough trustee of her beauty. She is blown in and out of my arms. She will have gone to snort coke in someone's flat. She will come back and throw herself over me, imagining I find the combination of flaking face powder and cigarette-flavoured perfume erotic. (I do.) I will stare through her skin and bones into another galaxy. She will

*bury her face in my neck and allow a few tears to
trickle into my ear.*

Sara's small, maddeningly perfect face appeared in the
glossy monthlies. David Bailey shot her. Older men
wanted to protect her and fuck her. I don't know whether
she loved me or was capable of loving *anybody*, but for a
young man a little narcissistic elevation goes a long way.
In bed, with my mouth on her mouth, I felt as loved and
held as I'd ever felt in my life. Did she think I was a troubled soul, a lost boy she could help to find himself? Not
even that, I suspect. As she weighed her options, fixed her
gaze on grander prizes, I was a mere stage in an ascent,
nothing more. And yet I was helplessly gripped by the
excruciating need to have her to myself.

For a year we co-habited in the basement flat, apparently happy, she occasionally dragging me to gatherings
where the complacently rich converged with the painfully
hip. She sat at some vortex of fashion, aristocracy and
New Romanticism. The theme song of the hour was 'Ashes
to Ashes', and there were pirates and dandy highwaymen
everywhere around us. Bowie's song, with its video featuring the epicene Steve Strange, was also the musical theme
of a week Sara and I spent with Antony in the South of
France: that and Kraftwerk's glacially seductive 'The
Model', which I could not hear as anything other than a
painful warning: 'She's playing her game and you can hear
her say / She is looking good, for beauty we will pay . . .'

(Photo Duffy @ Duffy Archive)

I had no innate style and even less interest in clothes, so must have disappointed Sara terribly. At a time when I was beginning to write about pop music – it was Sara who'd dropped off some examples of my writing at *NME* in Carnaby Street – I felt quite at odds with the 'new sounds, new styles' issuing from Soho and Covent Garden. At twenty-one I was already nostalgic for the seventies and certainly ill prepared for the greedy, garish eighties.

Heroin itself was hopelessly *passé* in this brave new demi-monde of pantaloons and flouncy hair; everything was now *up*, not down and nodding out. But that was hardly enough to stop me using and needing the drug. Many were the nights when Antony came south of the river in a taxi, came like a doctor on callout with his medical bag. I would wait in tormenting suspense for the diesel rattle of the cab on the gravel drive outside, knowing that once he was in the house the first rush was only minutes away.

Exactly when Sara chose to join in I don't remember. Even after she had proffered her tiny veins for the first time she was far more careful than Antony or me. 'Just enough to get a little buzz,' she would say, knowing she had to rise early the next day for her job at a fashion magazine. After she'd gone to bed, Antony and I would sit together at a big dining table and shoot up and talk – conversation that accelerated manically when cocaine was added to the mix.

By 4 a.m. we are shooting more coke every 20 minutes. Antony says I am in an 'egoistic trance', but I am horrified, trying to draw myself out of his voice. Coke's volte-faces – moments of great calm, moments of intense depression – make me claustrophobic, as though imprisoned in the web of his speech. By documenting every problem and decision in his life he imagines he has stepped out of life altogether. I applaud the obsession of it, but I don't personally want to hear these things performed as a kind of tour de force. I cannot speak back against this voice. My only response is back here, afterwards. I cannot be his confessor.

One morning the world changed irrevocably. I awoke to find no Sara in the bed and instead a note on the dressing table in her artful handwriting. She asked me not to worry about the fact that she had 'gone away' for a few days: she would be back and everything would be as it was. But nothing was the same again, especially after I'd located the little journal she kept – why had she not taken it with her? – and discovered the phrase, 'L., I need you now' in its latest entry. It was a mute appeal that stabbed my heart and froze me with horror. I had not known that you could be forsaken, betrayed by the very person who had saved you. But then it's never very wise to ask a lover to save you in the first place.

I was helpless with fear, a child dragged from its mother. I was 'beside myself', unable to fathom what had happened or for how long I'd been duped. The ground fell from beneath me. Had Sara been with 'L.' in Paris on the weekend that I had been there to see the Saints, an Australian punk band to which Richard had earlier converted me? I tried to find out who L. was and where Sara had gone with him, my hurt matched by humiliation. Had I ever wanted to kill myself before that shocking morning? Not really. Not seriously.

At this exact point I became very serious about heroin. The world was merciless and you should, as Derek Jacobi counselled in *I, Claudius*, 'trust no one, my friend'. But you could trust smack. Smack routinely did what it said it would do: insulate you against the cold, stop time hammering at the door. On heroin I floated through the dark, sure that all would ultimately be well. I tried to ensure that I was never again left exposed to my feelings.

Outside my body as it lives in this state, everything is perfect and the future is stable. There is no pressure to feel anything besides plans for a future that will never come. I move from smack to codeine linctus and back without a moment's pain. But until I come to terms with my future – the emptiness I see spiralling ahead – I will never know real peace and order. Are these insights signs of hope? No, for they see nothing but drugs and model everything in their image – including love, which I may have turned into a drug when it needn't have been anything of the kind.

Sara came back as she'd said she would – from Milan, as it transpired – and I was almost able to believe she had been 'working something out' of her system. I even visited Luca, an aristocratic Italian photographer whose lens answered her narcissism, to determine how serious their dalliance was. Like some bumpkin *ingénu* who'd wandered into a remake of *Les Liaisons Dangereuses*

– or merely like the masochist I must have been – I sat in his Fulham flat and heard him out.

If you want to keep a woman, says swarthy fun-loving Luca, you have to play the game too. You can only keep her 'curious' by disappearing yourself. In contrast to my gloomy obsessive English passion he offers his casual Italian freedom: 'You can marry her now and she will leave you in two years, or you can play the game and have fun for five . . .' Grazie, Luca.

The Milan jaunt was but the first of a series of woundings. I began to live in a constant dread of losing Sara. How I long now to intervene in the lives of those who've been cheated on, to tell them there's no way back from such betrayal, that they should get out and not prolong an agony that will only increase and rob them of all dignity. At twenty-one, however, you cannot know this and no one will tell you – because you will not believe it. The prospect of being deprived of the beloved's presence, of being alone again, is too harrowing to bear.

• • •

On a Friday in March of 1981, Sara flew to New York as the guest of a wealthy admirer who was staying in a loft in the Garment District. I scrambled together enough money to fly out after her, a drowned rat of a jealous lover touching down at icy JFK in order to . . . what? Win her back? She hadn't even left me, she simply wanted a weekend in Manhattan that I could not pay for.

I had an ally in Antony, who was busy hunting oblivion in a dirty hotel near Madison Square Garden and helped execute a daring commando raid on the loft, just a few blocks north on 38th Street. For two nights, like Kerouac and the Cassadys, we three shared Antony's room at the Seville – Sara and me in the bed, Antony gallantly on the floor. Perhaps I should have offered to share her with him as he'd once shared a girl with me. Some years later they shared each other anyway, though he seemed to take her more in his stride than I ever could.

We traipsed about an arctic Manhattan, shuffling through the Frick Museum on opium and gawping at the Watteaus and Fragonards. We saw the young Prince play a spectacular show at the Ritz, complete with garters, jock-straps and suspender belts. (The miniature Minneapolitan would become, for me, the true redeemer of the soulless decade we now found ourselves in.) The next day, Sara flew back to London.

I remained in my city of rock dreams and made a pilgrimage to the lair of Lester Bangs, a sea of vinyl on a noisy and unprepossessing block of Sixth Avenue south of 14th Street. That most unfettered and free-associative of American rock critics welcomed me graciously and seemed to appreciate the attentions of a pipsqueak fanboy from London.

Lester is unhappy but believes suicide is a waste of time – and says as much in one of his 'No Wave country-and-western' anthems. He tapes for me his terrible album with the Delinquents. We agree on the stupidity of the NME, which has seen fit not to run the recent pieces he's recently submitted. We are, after all, talking about the only great writer on pop music ever.

As I navigated the waves of albums scattered across his floor, Bangs evangelized about recent releases by Mars, DNA and – his special favourites – Teenage Jesus & the Jerks. These scratchy, dissonant recordings were a world away from Television and 'Chinese Rocks' yet remained

Lester (left) holds forth
(Tom Hill/WireImage/Getty Images)

of a piece with the too-cool-to-care blankness of their CBGB forebears. A little over a year later, Lydia Lunch of the Jerks called me in London to say Lester had died in that apartment, sealing his reputation as the most rock star of all rock journalists.

Lester wasn't a junkie but he was afflicted by addiction and actively seeking recovery at the time of his death. 'I suspect almost every day that I'm living for nothing,' he'd written. 'I get depressed and I feel self-destructive and a lot of the time I don't like myself . . . But I also feel that this precarious sentience is all we've got and, simplistic as it may seem, it's a person's duty to the potentials of his own soul to make the best of it.'

Lester could not have guessed that, only the night before I met him, I'd been down to the Lower East Side's notorious Alphabet Jungle with Antony to buy a bindle of bad heroin and a used works, returning to the Seville to inject the drug and pass out on the floor. He wouldn't have cared that I came to New York again that September in the company of a raggle-taggle band of Australians, three of whom shared my appetite for smack. This gothic post-postpunk quintet, known (after Harold Pinter's play) as the Birthday Party, had become my personal rallying cry in London, kicking violently as they did against pop's synthetic pricks in a one-band Dionysian insurrection. Their concerts were crazed and unpredictable irruptions of the Id at a time when smarmy telegenic Ego counted for everything. Nor could it have been more uncool that they were using heroin, that most 'rockist' of all substances and a sorry signifier of discredited seventies decadence.

In my *NME* piece about the group I wrote that

in this Apollonian climate of cold design and concealed despair, the Birthday Party take the concept of stage performance about as far as you are likely to see it go. Live, the songs of singer Nick Cave and guitarist Rowland Howard are driven to an emotional edge where pain and pleasure fuse – in cathartic madness for the performer and dithyrambic joy for the audience. Their concerts are feasts of energy, chaotic spectacles that break the surface of art and carry sound and lyric to ultimate violence. If Captain Beefheart or Pere Ubu seem too quirkily surreal, the Birthday Party in performance burst through the constrictions of intellect to a 'raw power', that original sin which Iggy Pop so rightly perceived as 'laughing at you and me . . .'

I cleaved to the Birthday Party as keepers of the flame that Iggy had lit on the Stooges' incendiary 1970 album *Fun House*, championing them in the face of snickering from *NME* peers who – actively nurturing a British 'New Pop' sensibility that grouped together everybody from ABC to Orange Juice – declined to take Antipodeans seriously. Providing moral encouragement from Australia itself was Richard, who'd returned to his native Sydney to work for

Cave Man: The Birthday Party live
(Bleddyn Butcher/REX/Shutterstock)

Rupert Murdoch and who even snuck into the pages of *The Australian* the single most outlandish album review I have ever seen in a national newspaper. I must assume the Digger did not so much as skim-read this piece on *Prayers on Fire*, but Richard mailed me a photocopy I have kept to this day. 'This music,' he'd written, 'was cut from love for the body which decays and sex which is enlightened by death. Its secret message is that time is short and all should be pleasure.'

Sara came to see a number of bands with me, but I do not recall her seeing the Birthday Party. In any case, our relationship was coming to a stop if not a definitive terminus. I'd survived another humiliating pursuit of the errant beloved, following her out to Florence and trying to establish which *palazzo* she was secreted in with her photographer.

Coming here has made the pain so much worse. The smack has run out, so there's nothing to take off the vicious edge of abandonment. Aside from the odd exhibition – Dubuffet at the Palazzo Medici Ricardo, Joseph Cornell at the Palazzo Vecchio – Florence's splendours, crawling with vermin in sunshades, attest only to the melancholy fate of humanism. I am not going to be just another one who 'got hurt' in love. If she does not love me, that is the end of it. If I have been so completely deceived, then life goes quickly down the drain. I cannot picture her, yet I know the shape of her body and my memory caresses it. I imagine her lover's body as my own wastes away.

Back in London it became clear it wasn't Luca I should have been worrying about but another rival, this time from within the ranks of the English upper crust. James had it all: looks, money, cocaine and a large duplex flat on the Fulham Road. What chance for an impoverished pop journo with a heroin habit and a damp basement south of the river.

Some small shred of self-preservation now surfaced in me: there was a 'last straw' that had me evicting Sara from the basement and even, wretch that I was, driving her belongings up to James's flat. But that still wasn't the end of it. Try as I might to 'let go' of my faithless siren, I remained addicted to her touch and her supplications. Another man might have simply replaced her with heroin, but there are few more potent chemicals in this world than sexual obsession. I thought of her and wrote of her and attempted to dislodge her from my frantic mind.

Addicted to her limbs, my own survive only through smack. Since my body no longer supports itself, my mind has begun to feed on it and will destroy it unless heroin is at home to guard it. Antony says to summon the Pretorian guard – but how to rescue myself from the memory of her body?

This is what a broken heart is, at least for a boy in the body of an Oxbridge graduate who reads too much into the world and endlessly seeks validation in the words of others. Richard, who'd tutored me in so much, supplied reading lists. Any study of doomed obsessive love, preferably French, became a sacred text. Roland Barthes' *A Lover's Discourse* was a bible ('I have projected myself into the other with such power that when I am without the other I cannot recover myself'). From Maurice Blanchot's *Gaze of Orpheus* I took the notion that Sara was my Eurydice ('the desire which leads Orpheus to see Eurydice and to possess her, while he is destined only to sing about her'). From André Breton and Georges Bataille came themes of elusiveness and horror that I feverishly scrawled in notebooks. Cocooned by heroin, I smiled as I noted down the transgressive *aperçus* of these men. The next day, shivering from withdrawal and lacking cash to score, I found scant consolation in the notes.

> *No more drugs please, but then no more of any-thing. The last weeks have been an undreamlike nightmare. I see nothing taking shape in the trajectory of my future. I cannot write or even think anymore. I burn with shame at my fail-ings. To live in the beauty of doubt, to be unable not to feel – what I wouldn't give for that. But the terrible courage it will take to go on and not look back ... I wonder whether I shouldn't simply kill myself today. I have no one, there is no comfort left, not the remotest hope, only a dreadful silence – my body alone, my existence unknown to another person. But no: if I wait, I will simply see her again. One more night of love and then death.*

Throughout the harsh winter of 1981–1982 I made daily excursions from Clapham to Hampstead to score from a ferocious Gorgon in a huge house off Haverstock Hill.

My Chemical Romance

One night my car wouldn't start and sat for weeks in North London encrusted with snow.

It was snow, too, that betrayed me to my parents after I'd somehow dragged myself up to Suffolk for Christmas. The cancelling of Boxing Day trains back to London brought on withdrawals in front of my mother and father as I sat wrapped in a tatty overcoat before a crackling fireplace. The truth was forced out of my sister, who'd seen me shoot up in Clapham. Repeated use of heroin had increased the production of μ-opioid receptors in my brain, leading to dependence, spasms, intense anxiety and severe insomnia.

Appalling weakness, inertia from withdrawal. My legs throb with exhaustion. Notwithstanding Night Nurse and other sedatives, I have not slept for three nights. I want to sink down and never have to clamber up again. The twin, interchangeable addictions to S. and to drugs must be given up at all costs. An uncontrollable nausea comes over me, a feeling that I am this addiction and there's nothing left to survive it. I don't know if I can pass through this hell and forget. I don't know what could lie beyond it or beyond the memory of her. I am terrified of getting stuck somewhere, or just stuck in drugs.

In the new year my parents dragged me to see a doctor in Knightsbridge, a man already steering posh junkies towards the Broadway Lodge treatment centre in Weston-super-Mare. The doctor pressed into my hands an American paperback entitled *Anger*, a gift that enraged me. I made a token phone call to a patient of his I'd known at Oxford, but failed to turn up at the appointed time to meet the reformed reprobate in question. I simply wasn't ready to admit defeat.

My father later confessed he'd simply assumed I would die, in hindsight the most sensible tack to take. There was no legacy of addiction in his family, but he knew enough about heroin to regard it as a virtual death sentence. I was still alive, however, when some months later he received a knighthood at Buckingham Palace and I stood beside him in a borrowed suit for the photograph, a packet of smack snug in the pocket of my jacket.

Like Rilke's prodigal son, I do not want my family's love. I only want her body again. In a waiting room I saw her in a magazine – more gorgeous and ravishable than ever.

To this day I'm unsure what others knew or guessed of my condition. To a fellow addict, the pinned pupils and undernourished limbs would have made it transparent. At *NME* I kept it quiet, sometimes fixing in the Carnaby Street toilets but never flaunting it to colleagues who deemed heroin to be deeply outmoded and who were additionally, I suspect, perplexed by me and by my writing. Perhaps word got about after I was driven up to Liverpool to interview Echo & the Bunnymen by their manager Bill Drummond, only to go into severe withdrawal as I checked into my hotel. Other such *NME* trips were now routinely accompanied by heroin use.

> *This morning I shot up in Victoria Station. Tonight I stand looking up at Cologne Cathedral, here to interview a humourless group called Killing Joke. It's obscene that when I am drugged in this way I can believe Sara loves me. Ah, the peace that comes from shutting down the body's demands, setting the mind free in a timeless flight . . .*

I remember the *NME* lending its support to the Anti-Heroin Campaign, a hypocritical initiative endorsed by pop stars whose careers were already being derailed by drink and cocaine. Heroin was the *bad* drug, while cocaine was as acceptable as cappuccino. Don't even get me *started* on alcohol.

•   •   •

'Rock stars are not our friends . . .' Thus spoke the late Philip Seymour Hoffman as he did his mannered turn as

Lester Bangs in Cameron Crowe's *Almost Famous*. (It's a wise saying that Lester's *Creem* colleague Jaan Uhelszki reminded me of – since it was to her that Bangs had spoken it – when I later quizzed her about life on the road with Led Zeppelin.)

Bangs was right, and had it not been for heroin I might never have befriended my beloved Australians in the way I did. The Birthday Party weren't the friendliest people anyway, though I enjoyed talking about music with them. They were savage about all British groups save the Fall, reserving particular vitriol for the likes of Echo & the Bunnymen. They had a strange ganglike humour, dark and deadpan, that I never quite tuned into. They were gloriously chaotic – literally unmanageable – and only made it to their sporadic performances because of Mick Harvey, the fierce mother hen of the group.

Booed off the stage in New York, in London they began to attract a following of black-clad gothlings, patrons of the Batcave and other such dungeons. These weren't fey fans of the Cure but feral creatures prowling for danger, looking to be provoked in the way Iggy Pop had picked fights with bikers in Michigan. Few were the shows I saw that did not involve Nick Cave smashing some prat over the head with a microphone stand. After the gigs we'd repair to someone's squat – or to my Clapham flat – and shoot heroin. After that I'd compose another fervent article about them, usually referencing

Bataille (or Artaud or Dostoyevsky) and patiently explaining how they were laying waste to everything else in pop culture.

My life has become rather vague, due in part to the wilting presence of Rowland Howard. Tonight we are trying to pull ourselves together with the help of some linctus. Rowland has written a superb song for the next Birthday Party album called 'Several Sins'. Another, 'She's Hit', suggests something alto-gether more despairing has entered their lives . . .

It's hard to know how astonishing the group were or weren't: Nick Cave never forgave me for later stating that all my pieces about them had been written 'under the influence'. The fact remains that if you wanted to go on a death trip with a rock band, they were the only game in town. Moreover, their records and concerts distracted me from heartbreak at a time when Sara never quite put me out of my misery.

I am happy now because I could die. She is curled in my bed, she whose dreams I live through every waking moment. We have been sparring all night with H and C, playing the one off against the other until both spoke in the blood of one thing alone – the insanity of my love.

If I couldn't let go of her, she couldn't let go of my torment, gratified that she could still make the poor boy demented with desire.

What is this love if not a disease? How do people go on when they've known this intensity? I cannot bear to see the reflection of my deserted, unloved face. We are spinning away from each other, her every gesture a blithe whitewash of the pain she sees in me. The agony is not part of her; I am speaking to myself. She does not wish to be stopped in her tracks and shown the damage she's done. And this is the girl I chose to rescue me from the icy straits of solitude! Why must we come into this mad knowledge of possession? She never was mine.

One afternoon I took a train to see her at her mother's house in Surrey, making love to her on a chair in the chintzy sitting room. The next day I took the train back to London and could not stop sobbing the whole way home, more tears than I thought a person could contain. Were they tears of acceptance that I'd never properly have her again, or the expression of a greater grief even than that?

The experience of weeping, of emptying, and the blurring of sight: do these not betray some strange love of pain?

It shocked me that I could cry on that train before total strangers; that I couldn't stop even as I slunk back to the flat in Paddington I'd moved into. Yet perhaps it was also the start of healing. The tears were followed by yet another withdrawal: the sweet deep sleep one experiences before cold turkey, on this occasion terminated by an involuntary orgasm that jolted me awake in the late afternoon.

The only way I can ease the pain is to take this drug. It's the only thing that performs the miracle. The heroin must not run out, because the moment I start to feel again – to feel my body shake with longing for hers – I know nothing save the agony of her absence.

The Paddington flat was a junkie crash pad *par excellence*. Nick Cave and his girlfriend Anita – picture Jeanne Moreau fused with Rickie Lee Jones – occupied the only proper bedroom. Other strays camped out where they could. I got to sleep in Katherine's queen-size bed on the tacit understanding that I would, when capable, penetrate her as others slumbered around us in sleeping bags. For a short period we had our own dealer, the Iranian Parviz, on the floor with his Scottish girlfriend. Parviz's heroin was reliable and often so strong that Nick once nodded out over a candle, his mass of dyed black hair instantly igniting as he sat at the kitchen table. (I reached him in the nick of time with a kitchen towel.)

Go Johnny Go
(Richard Young/REX/Shutterstock)

At large in London at this time was Johnny Thunders, eking out a hand-to-vein existence in the company of fellow ex-New York Doll Jerry Nolan. Both are long dead now, though they limped on for more years than anyone could reasonably have expected. Thunders' shows were sloppy but irresistible to anyone ensnared by smack. He was Keith Richards without the money or much of the talent, teetering on the verge of unconsciousness as he peeled off raucous Gibson riffs and paid twisted tribute to his Noo Yawk forebears. A highlight was his camp stab at the Shangri-Las' 'Give Him a Great Big Kiss', a set-piece in which little JT – as hetero as they came, to the extent that he still possessed a libido – smooched either Nolan or bassist Tony James or that other hopeless dope fiend Stevie New.

That Thunders was pitiful was unarguable, yet I was mesmerized by the anachronism he represented and pitched a piece to *NME*'s deputy editor, who was only mildly amused when I later submitted an expenses claim for a quarter-gram of heroin – the only way I could persuade Johnny Boy to talk to me.

Twenty years later, when *Dazed and Confused* magazine reunited me with Nick Cave in his adopted Hove, I quoted to him a lyric from the brand-new Bad Seeds album *Abbatoir Blues* – lines that name-checked Thunders in a long list of incongruous icons. With a touch of adolescent blasphemy he'd placed Johnny after St John of the Cross, though he also misidentified him as the author of 'Chinese Rocks'. I asked Nick if he remembered the sunny Sunday on Westbourne Terrace when Thunders came to tea – or at least to shoot up the very strong smack I'd scored from Parviz. He replied that it had been one of the unforgettable moments of his life, not least because he himself had all but overdosed on the cotton bud Thunders had left in his spoon. 'I don't remember *much* about it,' he added, 'except that his hands were in unbelievably bad condition. But I wouldn't trade that moment for anything.'

As they do in such circumstances, things progressively worsened in Paddington. Periodically I managed to stop using heroin.

I'm off dope, clean and conscious. Me and my mate smack, we had a pact but it's broken. And here's the third night without a minute's sleep, though I ran myself into the ground in Hyde Park. I'm so tired I can barely move.

Purchasing large bottles of sweet green methadone from Rowland Howard's tiny girlfriend temporarily weaned me off the needle but could not remove the core craving for opiates. I'd replaced my natural endorphins with synthetic counterparts and could not get back to where I'd started. Even when, through sheer force of whatever willpower I retained, I managed to put distance between me and the drug, the moment inevitably came when I was again help-less in the face of the need to free myself of my Self.

The anticipation of junk, with nothing beyond it: in a few hours all will be remedied. Junk will take care of me.

Ironically it was on one of Richard's reading lists that I discovered the great Gregory Bateson, who in a breakthrough 1971 essay had identified alcoholism with the false epistemological reification of the Self. 'I shall argue,' Bateson had written, 'that the "sobriety" of the alcoholic is characterized by an unusually disastrous variant of the Cartesian dualism, the division between Mind and Matter, or in this case, between conscious will, or "self", and the remainder of the personality.'

I was far from ready, however, to comprehend what Bateson meant, preferring to seek a rationale for self-destruction in the writings of unrepentant junkies. I even scored pure heroin ampoules from Alexander Trocchi, the American author of smack classic *Cain's Book* and one of the last London addicts to be prescribed such luxuries.

Desperately I tried to turn torment into words that might redeem the squalor of my everyday life. At a certain point you have to glorify your drug use in order to bear it, to look at the creature wasting away in the mirror and think, 'You're so cool.' At that moment you are playing a part, spectating on your own slow implosion.

For *NME* I even wrote – and had published – a histrionic manifesto flagged up on the cover as 'Twilight of the Idols: Why Rock Stars Must Die' and largely inspired by Nietzsche's *The Birth of Tragedy from the Spirit of Music*. In it I wrote such deranged things as:

> I pay no more credence than anyone else to a life
> of wanton hedonism, but I know that in certain
> instances – those, let us say, in which the media has

altogether killed off or sterilized the mysteries of beauty and passion – debauchery is the single ally one has against the pervasion of normality. Vice, as Sartre said, is a taste for failure. Against the blinding light of rationality, adaptation, survival, we have only the solace of darkness.

To this day I can't believe that such pernicious propaganda wasn't spiked, especially when pop's prevailing flavour was so clean and hygienic – so *pro-life*. (When even Nick Kent dismisses your ravings as 'half-baked eulogies to self-destruction', you know you've gone too far.) I sought death everywhere in music: in deep soul, in Joy Division, in the acrid beauty of Billie Holiday's voice. Yet I also knew that music, even as it wallowed in pain, healed the heart. I cried deep tears as I listened to the Band's 'Whispering Pines', broke into pieces as Jessye Norman sang 'Im Abendrot', the last of Strauss's *Four Last Songs*. In those moments, death appeared as the sweetest relief.

All is lost: 'I can feel you standing there,' Richard Manuel sings, 'but I don't see you anywhere . . .' I cannot find my way out of this labyrinth, since everything leads back to some glimpse of perfect beauty, now withdrawn indefinitely. My thoughts of S. turn over themselves endlessly like waves. When I speak to others I see them strain to register

themselves in the void around me. I sense their
fear of this shell of being and do not want to hear
their futile platitudes. The longer I'm away from
that innocent harlot, the more stretched and taut is
my yearning, as though the cord between us could
never snap but only continue to stretch until it tore
out my insides.

•   •   •

In the summer of 1982 a call came from California. My
friend Mark, who I'd met through Antony, was staying
for no very good reason in Menlo Park, a CIA hub in
the heart of Silicon Valley. Ignorant of just how far I'd
sunk in London but perhaps intuiting my unhappiness,
he suggested I fly over for a visit.

I shall go to America. I shall decimate this desola-
tion. The thought of flight from this mess begins to
animate me.

Secreting a bottle of methadone in my hand luggage,
I threw clothes and books into a case and got the fuck
out of England, certain I could no longer live in the same
country as Sara and praying my drug use might cease
or at least mutate into something manageable were I
six thousand miles away from her. Later I learned that

this conceit was known as a 'geographical': the mad idea that when I landed at SFX I would not be lying in wait for myself. But wherever I went, there I was. Menlo Park was no different, especially after Mark flew east for a fortnight and left me with little besides a handful of triggering singles like Iggy's 'I'm Sick of You' and Sam Dees' 'Signed Miss Heroin'.

I am alone in America. I cannot adjust to the insane scale of the place. Without smack the world is naked. I think of Dion coming off his habit while listening to Robert Johnson: 'You may bury my body, down by the highway side . . .'

The methadone rapidly ran out and I went into prolonged withdrawal barely alleviated by beer and bourbon. For two weeks I slept not a wink, remaining sane only by watching ancient flickering B-movies on Mark's black-and-white television. If I was lucky I got *Gilda* or *Double Indemnity*, *noir* masterworks I'd seen with Richard at the Electric in London. More often I had to shiver through hearty Westerns and turgid melodramas, or just *Marcus Welby, M.D.*

I'm beginning to smell like a corpse. As I sweat off the last residues of heroin, it becomes difficult to share my own bed.

The author, California, June 1982
(Muir Mackean)

By day I attempted to activate a career as unofficial West Coast correspondent for *NME*, clattering the stiff keys of my typewriter in Mark's backyard, venturing into San Francisco in a gigantic old Dodge he'd acquired.

As I had with Lester Bangs, I cold-called Greil Marcus, whose book *Mystery Train* had so shaped my notions of American music, and in whose professorial company I saw an amusing punk group called the Descendents.

If anyone could get any heroin to me in this baking outpost it would be rather marvellous. To accept addiction to that innocent poison – to resign oneself to its programme – is really too awful. Yet part of the toll it takes is the steady erosion of the will. How can one talk of willpower when this sickness lies at the very heart of the will?

Unwittingly, *NME* paired me with a photographer who, unprompted, confessed a taste for 'Persian Brown' heroin and with whom I now began using the drug again. Chick was a scurrilous if likable rogue with a southern drawl who also appreciated the heady pleasures of intravenous cocaine use. In London, coke had made me disembodied and uneasy; now, in San Francisco, it became a consuming obsession, the white-light counterpart to sleepy brown smack.

Where heroin wrapped me in a warm eiderdown – loved me as I couldn't love myself – cocaine triggered braingasms that made me overlord of all I surveyed. The drug bound itself to the dopamine transporter in my brain, blocking the removal of dopamine from my synapse and producing a brief but intensely blissful signal to my receiving neurons. Sadly, as the many millions of freebasers and crackheads on the planet know, the ecstatic omnipotence of the first hit was followed by rapidly diminishing returns. Chasing the initial bliss would leave

me, hours later, terrified and suicidal, my arms a battle-
field of puncture marks.

Cocaine is an ever-icier solitude – the acid trip of
the blind man, pure consciousness turned in on
itself. Every rush is the final silence, but a marathon
coke session is the compression of a lifetime's smack
addiction. I do not think I am flesh anymore. I am
made of marble.

At least I could look at Chick's friend Tiffany – who
provided most of our coke – and believe I wasn't in such
shocking shape. She must once have been a pretty girl;
I even lay chastely in bed with her after one of those
marathon sessions. But she'd wasted away to skin and
bone. It would be a miracle if she were alive today.

One night I was using with Chick and Tiffany on Post
Street when she casually mentioned that Sly Stone had, only
the night before, stopped by to score from her. By chance
I'd just acquired an original copy of Sly & the Family
Stone's *There's a Riot Goin' On* in a store in Palo Alto, the
album quickly becoming the soundtrack to my Californian
cocaine compulsions. I'd also devoured the Sly chapter in
Marcus's *Mystery Train* and now listened repeatedly to
Riot and 'Thank You (Falettinme Be Mice Elf Agin)' as tes-
timonies to ghetto psychosis: 'Lookin' at the devil, grinnin'
at his gun . . .' If God put poppies on earth for pain relief,
only Satan could have created the coca plant.

Sly and the Family
(Everett/REX/Shutterstock)

With the omnipotence came the worst paranoia. That same night on Post Street we heard rumbling footsteps overhead and knew for sure the cops were about to bust Tiffany. In a crazed panic we flushed her drugs and hid the paraphernalia where we could. But if it was the SFPD on the roof, it was somebody else they were after. (I was lucky to have had so few scrapes with the law. On 26 November 1981, I was driving down the Earl's Court Road with Nick Cave as my passenger when a police car pulled us over and yanked us off to the local station for full-body cavity searches. They never found the tiny stash I'd jammed inside my *London A–Z*, but Nick had to stump up £100.)

Surreally, it turned out that the unassuming bungalow Mark was renting in Menlo Park belonged to a retired narc. Rooting about in his garden shed one afternoon, I came upon a cabinet packed with files on dozens of addicts arrested in the Bay Area over the previous decade. These were the hardest of the hardcore: men and women with convict faces impassively staring down the camera, the guys with names like Earl or Dale, the girls – prostitutes for the most part – called Shelley or Yolanda. There were dozens of them in the files and I wondered what had become of them. How many were incarcerated and how many dead? I half-expected to see Sly Stone among them but he'd eluded this particular narc. I looked at the brutalized faces and felt light years from London. What was a middle-class Oxbridge graduate doing shooting coke all night on Post Street? How had he got here and was there any way back?

Another binge this week, from which I'm only just recovering. I've taken stock of my irremediable poverty and see no solution to it. Perhaps I'll starve to death in some North Beach motel without notifying a soul of my whereabouts. Then again I could approach life for the first time with survival in mind . . .

For most addicts an alarming moment comes when you use with a friend who, it turns out, is *not* an addict – not that you frame it in those terms while it's happening. This moment came for me with Mark, who was game for the occasional speedballing session in Menlo Park but who could take drugs and then leave them – could turn in at 2.30 a.m. while there were still powders in the packets we'd scored.

'I think I'll hit the sack,' were Mark's words. Hearing them was a lonely moment for a needle freak who knew he *couldn't* turn in – who had to push on until all the powders were gone. It was tough at that point to sidestep the glaring evidence that my lust for drugs was different from his, as it had been different from Sara's. Mark must have felt the same sensations as the drugs entered his bloodstream, but those sensations were less essential to him than they were to me. He was not a laboratory rat, but I was. And I was still so far from admitting I was in the grip of something I could not control.

I cannot stand the cage that holds me a day longer. Wherever I go, I cannot enter life. I cannot keep waiting like this, waiting for the obliteration of my body.

It amazes me that I managed to work at all in that period. So often I was a whisker away from jeopardizing everything. One night Chick and I fixed coke till dawn and only just made a flight to Minneapolis to interview the ghastly Survivor, then perched at No. 1 with the *Rocky* theme song 'Eye of the Tiger'. Once in the Twin Cities we only just made it to the interview after sleeping off the previous night in our hotel rooms. No longer could I write without the bare minimum of heroin in my system.

Mark must, I think, have been relieved to see the back of me as I moved from Menlo Park to Chick's apartment on Polk Street. He'd soon return to London to continue growing up, while I would remain in California and regress into ever more perilous dependency. I had no clear idea where to turn and no money to turn ideas into plans. I figured if I hung around Tiffany and Chick for much longer I would die. Then again, I thought it might not be the worst thing in the world if I died anyway.

Perhaps it's better for me to be dead than to be condemned to living with myself like this.

There was a bleak Sunday in September 1982 when I felt completely alone in the world and devoid of all hope. (Funny how, decades later, one recalls specific days. Sundays are always the loneliest days in the junkie's calendar, though even these are trumped by weekday mornings when regular folk tramp the streets to work as you wipe the blood from your massacred veins.) The next day, however, I was rescued by a girl who flew up to San Francisco and took me down to Los Angeles, where I'd first met her with Chick when the three of us attended the first US Festival near San Bernardino.

Tanya was a sweet caretaker of a rock chick who liked wounded English boys and wanted to save them. She'd been raised in the desert paradise of Palm Springs, where her dad drove a Jaguar. He'd set her up in a small apartment at the foot of Nichols Canyon with Hollywood Boulevard whooshing past the windows, and I moved in without so much as a hint of protest.

When I was in New York last year it was Lester Bangs on life below 14th Street. Now it's gonzo king Richard Meltzer on the 'absolute nowheres' of L.A., 'just another base of operations in the void . . .'

I could not make myself fall in love with Tanya, since I didn't believe I would ever love anyone but Sara. She seemed to accept this as she accepted that I had no immediate plans to grow up. I lacked the shame not to take advantage of her goodness.

My guardian angel wonders if I am not the devil incarnate. She does not see that those who are most cruel are those who've glimpsed the highest happiness.

For a period I moderated my heroin use by replacing it with daytime drinking. Tanya would drive to her job at the Beverly Center and I'd drink cheap beer in front of her television set, flipping between soap operas and the newly launched MTV channel, most of whose videos seemed to consist of bushy blondes – of both sexes – reclining against the bonnets of red convertibles.

The early eighties was not a propitious time to be writing about pop. Bogus new wave ruled the airwaves in Los Angeles, which could muster only sociopathic suburban punk and fey Paisley Underground psych-pop in response. From time to time I was functional enough to borrow Tanya's steel-blue BMW and wend my way down the Harbor Freeway to San Pedro or Hermosa Beach to interview angry young bands on Slash or SST Records.

Black Flag live
(Jim Steinfeldt/Michael Ochs Archives/Getty Images)

Occasionally *NME* dispatched me to Florida or the Midwest to file stories on American sensations of the day – pop trip of a lifetime: three days on the road with Prince – but the paper wasn't especially interested in Southern California, preferring Manchester to Malibu. Though it was scorned by Londoners and New Yorkers alike, I'd developed a perverse fondness for L.A. from my first visit in 1978. No less than Aldous Huxley or Christopher Isherwood or Reyner Banham, I loved the parching heat and plastic sprawl of it all. 'There is nothing more reassuring to someone who's gone through an acute identity crisis,' Philip K. Dick had written in 1972, 'than clean plastic apartments, streets, restaurants and furniture.'

A month ago I was so frightened I thought I had to die. Now it's mid-October, and every day I walk up to Wattles Park, a small oasis nestling in the hills, and Los Angeles becomes a mere blur of noise below. I am happy here, it's the sanctuary for which I longed. I must simply sink into this place and remain here. Tanya has been very good to me. For her it must be like harbouring a fugitive.

Peter Conrad had lectured at Oxford on Waugh's *The Loved One* and Isherwood's *A Single Man*, making me hanker for Hollywood Babylon in all its fraudulent fantasia. I enjoyed the sheer inappropriateness of the place for someone of my saturnine sensibility: the environment was a balm for torment. No more schlepping up to Hampstead on vicious winter afternoons, no more near-overdoses in Clapham or Paddington. If you're going to be a bum, be a bum in Santa Monica, where the vagrants all look like Christ on a catwalk.

I liked driving with Tanya to Palm Springs, where movie idols and lounge lizards went to die. One night we were living out some ersatz-Sinatra fantasy in her parents' rambling home on Via Vaquero when a sinister bubble appeared on a vein I'd just punctured. Somehow we got to the family doctor without Mom and Pop finding out. 'You been doing some of that joy-poppin'?' the doc said with a strange giggle. I guess he'd seen a few abscesses in his time.

Intermittently I tried to live a normal life, walking Tanya's dog, buying canned chilli at the 'Rock and Roll Ralph's' on Sunset. Sometimes I'd go with Tanya's sweet pal Dennis to Dodger Stadium and almost feel like a regular guy with my popcorn and Budweiser. But eating away at me all the while was a longing to fuck everything up again: no more quarter-grams of cut coke and scuzzy Mexican smack but a *grande bouffe* of speedball excess.

I'd been regularly corresponding with Richard, who was now in New York, and hatched a plan to meet him in London:

R.,

A syringe lies before me. I wish I could attribute the state of degradation and torpor in which I find myself to the obscure fascination you have always exercised over me. It was you who first opened the abyss into which my life has sunk.

You must meet Antony, the only being as disastrously decayed as you or me – and my sometime companion in the search for truth via drugs and destruction.

I think coke has fried all our brains. As Artaud said, that which is pure is always elsewhere.

B.

The idea was to obtain a lot of heroin and cocaine in London and kill ourselves. I don't know that I ever believed Richard was serious, and he may have assumed I would not go through with it either. If he'd proposed a genuine suicide pact at the house on Campden Hill Road, would I have signed on the dotted line? Probably not.

I went directly from Heathrow to Antony's flat in Cornwall Gardens, where Richard awaited me. I'd seen neither of them in months. The next three days were lost to a blizzard of cocaine psychosis only mildly allayed by the safety blanket of heroin. We barely slept. Antony came and went, bringing further supplies. I don't believe he was privy to our plan, which required leaving enough smack for one last terminal shot apiece.

My Chemical Romance

On the Monday morning I awoke to find that Richard had left without a word – flown back to New York as though the whole thing had been no more than an ironic jape.

•   •   •

I could so easily have died at this time. Addiction reduced me to such abject dependency. There were never enough drugs – or there was never enough *money* for drugs – to plug the leak in my soul.

Back on Nichols Canyon Road in early 1983, out of concern for Tanya if nothing else, I again tried to regulate my intake of Class A's. I even forsook heroin when, in March, the Birthday Party came to play the Roxy on Sunset Boulevard. With a visiting Chick in tow, I went to pay respects to the group at the infamous Tropicana Motor Hotel, where all out-of-town rockers put up. Surprised as Nick and Rowland were by my declining the pale brown line atop their TV set, I stuck to my guns and patted myself on the back, convinced that this time I had it licked.

Seeing the Birthday Party play in the plush club opened by über-moguls Lou Adler and David Geffen a decade earlier was all wrong, and they knew it. Angelenos understood U2 and New Order (and Modern English) but were bemused by these scabby Antipodeans, who didn't even bother to simulate the violence they'd

staged in London and New York. The band was almost over, in any case. Next time I saw Nick he was leading his new group the Bad Seeds, en route to a long and respectable career as an artist who would one day get his hour on *The South Bank Show*. Sometimes it's the most self-destructive ones who turn out to possess the most puritanical work ethic.

My resolutions never lasted long. An evening would come – or an afternoon, or a morning – when I again found myself unarmed against the hunger for drugs. And when I lacked money of my own I stole from Tanya, forging her signature on cheques I'd take to Joel the coke dealer, fifteen minutes east on Fountain Avenue. Or I'd haul a pile of promo albums down to Aron's Records and come away with enough cash to blast myself into orbit. Crack was not with us yet, but Joel's freebase pipe was enough to send me sky-high.

One grotesque night in June I returned from Joel's to find Tanya curled up on the sofa with a stack of bridal magazines. We hadn't had sex in weeks and now she wanted to marry me. As I lurched back and forth to the bathroom, inventing some fiction that I'd drunk gallons of water and needed to pee, I could only think, wretchedly, 'Let the poor girl believe what she wants; by the time she sets the wedding date I'll be dead.'

I do not want a guardian angel anymore. I bring only dread and ugliness into Tanya's life. It is she alone who prevents me from overdosing in the toilet.

The following Saturday I was gagging for smack when Tanya struck a deal: if Joel hadn't called by seven she would instead phone her musician pal Alex, who'd stopped using heroin and might be able to help me. I'd resisted help for so long that I scarcely took her seriously. But since she'd have been paying for the drugs, I had no choice but to agree. In agony I watched the clock tick towards seven. Nobody called. Seven came and I gave a resigned shrug.

Alex drove me to a big room – something like a church hall – in what Hollywood later drolly referred to as 'the slums of Beverly Hills'. For some years afterwards, as if it had been a magical place I'd hallucinated, I tried to work out where the room had been. Then one day I was walking along North Robertson Boulevard and straight-away knew the building where it had all begun for me, where I'd entered terrified as a child who would have done anything not to attend a birthday party. I cannot remember what was said in that room, other than a word ('God', or more accurately 'Gard') that made me think I was among born-again Californian Christians. It's possible Alex suggested I disregard the word; he hardly struck me as God-fearing himself.

I do know I heard men and women speak of drugging and drinking in terms that convinced me I was in the right place. And perhaps more important, I heard them speak of feelings – of the prompts for drugging and drinking – with an openness and acceptance I'd never encountered before. For all the differences I could point to, for all the laid-back Californianisms that grated with my British cynicism, I knew I was the same as these people: I was a lost soul with a serious problem I'd been unable to solve. In the same way that I'd come home to my own body via heroin – made some kind of physical peace with myself – I now came home to a power that was greater than my own vain efforts to stop using.

My habit at this point was not as great as it had once been, thus I did not need a supervised detox. Instead I got myself to other rooms and congregations. One was a men's group in a hospital, arranged around a long boardroom table. Another took place at a location later celebrated in the Afghan Whigs' song 'Fountain and Fairfax'. Still another was a group in Venice consisting of myself – a nine-stone Oxbridge graduate – and several heavy-set Hispanic ex-cons with tattooed biceps the size of hams. I don't know that I've felt so out of place any-where in my life.

Subsequently I've found myself in groups all over the world where the initial sensation was one of soci-ological estrangement: one in Manhattan that was all-African-American save for the tall balding figure of a well-known and very WASPy singer-songwriter; a roomful of bigoted-looking whites in a remote corner of northeast Alabama; a more or less exclusively gay men's group in New Orleans; a tiny huddle of sunburned expats in the Algarve; even a predominantly female gathering in New York's West Village. Strange bedfellows all, yet all of them brothers and sisters beneath the skin.

In the daytime I would sit in my little oasis in Wattles Park, Tanya's hound at my side, and – in a fever of false humility – write lists of those I'd harmed, not grasping that I was leapfrogging crucial stages of the way and was supremely unprepared for the business of repairing damage.

But I knew I had found what I'd so desperately been seeking. Perhaps the game was finally up.

PART 2
THE POOR LITTLE TENTACLES OF SELF

'. . . this is the reason why so often in free life one hears it said that man is never content. In fact, it is not a question of a human incapacity for a state of absolute happiness but of an ever-insufficient knowledge of the complex nature of the state of unhappiness.'

Primo Levi, *If This is a Man*

'I'll tell you a secret I've never revealed: however we are is okay.'

Judee Sill, 'Lopin' Along Thru the Cosmos'

The game, as it turned out, was not quite up. I returned to London, Tanya following close behind, and made the grave error of reconnecting with Antony.

In a replay of the original basement seduction, my old friend dropped into the conversation in Cornwall Gardens the fact that there was heroin on his person. Once the junk hunger was coursing through me he shook a line of sandy powder on to a sheet of foil and carried it to the window.

'Shall we let the wind take it?' he asked.

Minutes later I was opiated for the first time in weeks, which didn't stop me dragging Antony to his first recovery group in an evil-smelling hostel in the World's End. I spent most of the hour and a half nodding off in my seat, my head slowly sinking towards my breastbone before rearing up in sudden embarrassment – only to repeat the sorry process again moments later.

One of my first *NME* assignments on returning from

Viva Alan Vega
(Press Agency/REX/Shutterstock)

America was to go back there almost immediately – this time to a Manhattan foetid with August heat, specifically to a SoHo loft belonging to Alan Vega of my beloved Suicide. Vega was a sweetheart, a Brooklyn hustler reborn as an ageing icon of downtown transgression. Midway through our interview he produced a bag of cocaine from a drawer and I accepted the offer of a generous line. I simply hadn't learned that 'No, thank you' was the most important phrase in the recovering addict's lexicon.

I used cocaine again in Maryland, where I flew on to interview Talking Heads, then used more in Detroit in the merry company of P-Funk prankster George Clinton. The drug must have been visibly exiting my pores as I re-entered the UK on a sweaty Saturday morning, for I was led away at Heathrow and strip-searched for the first time since my detainment with Nick Cave on the Earl's Court Road.

In the late summer of 1983, when I was twenty-four, the penny dropped. My last drug use lacked glamour of any kind: it was a hasty swig from a bottle of kaolin-and-morphine in my grandparents' bathroom cabinet in West Bergholt, Essex, and achieved precisely nothing. But the next morning – 25 August 1983 – I awoke with enough shame and disappointment in myself to make it the highest priority not to use that day. I've been clean ever since, and every day it's been the single most important thing in my life that I did not allow a mood-altering drug to enter my body. Finally I was ready not merely to stop but to *stay* stopped.

In November, by a strange coincidence, I flew to Madrid to be a guest on a TV pop show featuring none other than Alan Vega. I greeted him warmly but when later he phoned my hotel room to say he was in possession of some 'really good stuff' I managed to reply that I was tired and needed sleep. It was as difficult and as simple as that, and the next morning I was able to amble about the Prado museum without feeling freaked out. Perhaps there was something in this staying-clean business after all.

Saying no for twenty-four-hour stretches became the central tenet of Life After Drugs. Like every junkie I ever knew, I'd regularly assured family and friends they would never see me stoned again, unaware that the hollow promise all but guaranteed I would slide back into a habit. Now, with the support of fellow recoverers, I could make sacred the simple stricture of not letting the first mood-altering chemical into my system for This Day. 'Tomorrow I may use, but not today.'

Cravings for the comfort of oblivion did not depart overnight. For months any strong feeling, good or bad, caused me to hallucinate giant syringes floating like zeppelins over London. But this was the point: that without drugs I would be free to have feelings I'd stifled, buried, displaced for years. Not that I wanted those feelings; not that I could identify or name those feelings. But I knew that I needed to have them, and that having feelings was probably what life was about.

To stop using is only the start of the solution. I have to fill the abyss that drugs carved out of my life.

When exactly had I *stopped* having feelings? Certainly before I took heroin the first time; arguably as far back as early childhood, when apparently innocuous but compulsive behaviours – obsessive collecting of toys and football cards – first came to my rescue. For I could now see that addictions were, first and foremost, protective repetitions designed to eliminate difficult choices, narrowing consciousness to something I could manage and even, temporarily, control.

The particular drug or behaviour was not the issue. It was the need not to feel that governed the using. And it may be the addict's specific immaturity that demands a life of seamless pleasantness with no discernible bumps in the road. Addicts maintain a fiction that they walk on the wild side when all they really want is to feel safe. With smack in me I'd felt indifferent to fate; without it I was naked and lacking at least one layer of skin. The first months of recovery were thus a purgatory of self-consciousness and self-loathing.

I feel so little confidence in talking of myself that I start to sweat the instant somebody asks what I do. I've been so ill-at-ease with everyone today. What am I not doing right? Yet it must be a good thing that I'm facing my fears and not running away. I suppose the miracle is that I don't want to use or booze; I merely want to evaporate.

I knew I had to bear the agony of discomfort. I did not know my place in the world and could not find a way to fit in with others. I dreaded going to the *NME* office because I didn't know how to be around others or *who* to be. It may be that such dread is usual for most twenty-four-year-olds, but *my* life depended on not seeking instant relief from the attendant anxiety. I could not drink with my colleagues, could not blur our differences with alcohol. I stood and sweated with the effort of it all, unaware that I did not have to hold my own with any other person on earth.

Nothing really matters except the matter of existence itself. We should be staring in wonder at each moment. Instead we regret yesterday and dread tomorrow, dumping on today as if it lacked all value. The intimacy of NOW is what we deny and distract ourselves from.

Along with not taking The First Drug, I had to resist The First Contact With Sara, who worked less than a hundred yards from the *NME* offices. I began to see that my addiction to her stemmed from the same emptiness that generated the need for drugs – paralleled and exacerbated it but could not substitute for it. Drug-free, I even began to demystify my obsession with her: to understand that, just as heroin addiction is not the property of the drug itself, so erotic obsession is the exclusive property of its subject.

Twice I ran into Sara in the company of a former coke dealer, herself now abstinent; twice I steeled myself to decline the implicit invitation to offer myself as a white knight. I was no white knight, merely a boy in a young man's body trying to assemble an authentic identity for himself.

If I'd known how long the journey to authenticity would take, would I have continued to trudge this road?

But I didn't know: had no idea, indeed, how much legitimate suffering lay ahead. I simply had to trust that not running from reality would change the way I saw the world. For the goal of all this was becoming clearer by the day: I needed to change into a person I could live with. To be in constant conflict with one's self was a hell on earth.

I could have been more honest had I told Tanya I would never love her enough to warrant her staying with me. Instead I waited for her to reach that conclusion herself. I don't know how much pain it caused her to get there, but the day came when she found enough worth in herself to return to California. I will always be grateful for her love and kindness.

For a long time afterwards I was too petrified of rejection to go near any woman I desired. Without drugs I couldn't find the words to say to girls. I regressed to the place I'd been in at Oxford, falling at a distance for someone who, like Sara, was short and dark and beautiful. When finally I summoned the courage to invite her to a gig she fell ill, losing her voice so that she could barely apologize on the phone for letting me down. I took it as a sign of rejection and backed off, yet continued to love her for months. (Was Sara the archetype for the physical type that pierced my heart, or did the archetype lie further back in my childhood, in a dark-haired Swedish *au pair* who'd loved me and then, without explanation, disappeared back to Västerås?)

Surviving feelings of rejection may be the sternest test for the abstinent addict, yet the pedestrian business of living presents challenge enough. Just waking to one's fears each day; lacking manageable structure to one's existence; feeling unsure how even to place one foot before the other – these were fundamental hurdles to overcome.

This is the hardest part. The being, the existing. The taking each moment as it comes. Knowing at least intellectually that there is no future. I do not know what it means to be here or to be anywhere.

At the root of the unease, moreover, lies something I do not even know: that I am looking at the world in the wrong way. I do not know that I am a part of it at all, have always assumed I am *apart* and acted accordingly. I am lonely and cannot admit it. I am angry and am barely aware of it. I believe others are bound to reject and refuse me, and thus rule myself out of contention. There are significant periods of depression, not helped by a man who claims loftily that 'depression is merely a disingenuous term for self-pity'. Through all of it I keep writing, as if that will stave off self-doubt. I do not know what I really want. I have never asked myself what I really want.

As part of the commitment to change I take a systematic look at my life and learn that I'm carrying a world of hurt and grievance and have never talked to anyone about any of it. Throughout my drug use, was I ever honest with another human being? Did I ever confess to another that 'I'm scared' or 'I'm lonely' or 'I'm hurting'? I never said such things to my family, so why would I have said them to Antony or Richard or Sara? Slowly I come to see that speaking the truth about my inner world will be critical to bearing the outer one. I need to know that my feelings do not make me a freak, and that others have them too.

• • •

In those first months I received regular praise from family and friends alike.

'You must be so strong.'

'You have such willpower.'

'We're so proud that you've beaten this thing.'

In vain did I try to explain that I'd done the exact opposite of beating this 'thing'. I had, in fact, lain down and let the 'thing' stomp all over me. In the end I'd taken off the gloves and climbed out of the ring altogether. Having encountered a perfect double bind – *I cannot live without drugs; I cannot take drugs anymore* – I was finally prepared to give up on my own willpower. This was not going to be about Will, and the power would have to come from outside – or more accurately from *around* me, from something of which I was now a small part.

I went back to the book that Richard had pressed on me five years before. 'The whole epistemology of self-control which his friends urge upon the alcoholic is monstrous,' Gregory Bateson had written in his essay. Reading it again, I understood that drugs had made it possible to feel at one with the world because they'd put me in a complementary (or harmonious) rather than symmetrical (or competitive) relationship with others. Trying to stay clean via willpower kept me in competition with my environment. Paradoxically, giving up the fight against my 'demons' – to employ that hoariest of addiction tropes – enabled me to start a new life of complementary relationship to what Bateson called 'the larger world'.

To this day I do not have a strong opinion as to whether addiction is or is not an 'illness'. I'm not even very interested in whether I was or wasn't born with it, though I'm quite sure I wasn't. What matters is the acceptance that I can't control or even moderate my use of mood-altering drugs. It is irrelevant how much addicts learn about themselves, how much soul-searching and healing they do or even what reparations they make to people they've hurt. Once I take the first drug – put the taper to the fuse of active addiction – it's inevitable that the gunpowder barrel will eventually explode.

To those who still, decades later, praise me and others for resisting temptation, I continue to argue it's not the Self that resists – that *I* have not had to 'fight this thing' for many years. I simply make the decision not to use for This Day – and to become part of Bateson's 'larger world'.

• • •

Question: how do you stay clean for over thirty years?

Answer: I don't. I stay clean for today or for this hour or for whatever unit of time I can manage. If the compulsion to score seems too great, that's because it is. It's too much for me to resist. But if it's Me + You it's different. Me + You is a greater force than the self-will that will always be defeated.

Whatever collective one is plugged into, this seems to be how it works: instead of calling the dealer or pouring the first glass of wine or whisky, I call *You*, someone who understands my frantic need to 'get out of my head'. Instantly, I connect to something that's bigger than me, and thus my load is lessened. We're in this together, for our survival depends on the bond we feel.

A few months into my recovery I registered this conscious thought: I could use today but it would feel like trampling over the heads of everyone who's helped me (as well as those I've tried to help). These friends now stand between me and the first drug, and they're better for me than any drug will ever be. Even if I sit at the back of the room and feel terror at the prospect of engaging with others, something is happening here that I can't rationally explain. I'm hearing the struggles and solutions of people who react to life as I do, who are trying to heal as I am trying to heal – and it's changing me.

Do I believe a word any of them say? Can I trust that they're being honest? Maybe not, but isn't it better to be let down than never to trust at all? The evidence before me suggests there are people who've stopped using and stayed stopped; who, moreover, have begun to live in ways that would once have been unthinkable; who've been able to engage with the world as it is and found peace and purpose in doing that.

It's true I do not care for every person in these rooms. Some reflect my own ingrained tendencies to avoid and evade – to act out – though I do not even realize this is why I don't like them. However, there are enough who possess something I want: a measure of self-acceptance and self-respect, a willingness to be human and reveal themselves as flawed and fallible. I'm so reluctant to reveal myself as I really am, because it leaves me feeling open to attack. Yet I feel no desire to attack others who make themselves vulnerable, who voice their pain and confusion. I seem only to feel love for such people.

It will take years to trust that I will not repel you by speaking my uncomfortable truth, such is my investment in your seeing me as sorted. But I'm more trusting than I was, less quick to presume my mistakes are proof of a general failure that others will judge harshly.

• • •

Question: What does it mean to have stayed clean for over thirty years?

Answer: It may mean nothing more than that I'm drug-free for this day. In itself it is no guarantor of happiness or sanity. A crack addict three days off the street may be saner than I am if I've lost my connection to my fellows and the spiritual principles I live by. In abstinence I still go to dark places where there's no comfort and kinship, where ego reigns in Warren Zevon's 'splendid isolation'. (Read Crystal Zevon's account of her ex-husband's self-willed seventeen-year sobriety for a salutary study of white-knuckle abstinence.)

On the other hand it would be false humility to dismiss the benefits of accrued time in recovery, to claim I haven't gained more each time I've faced the unopposable reality of my life and gone through pain without using or killing myself. When I've ridden things out, trusted the pain will pass, I've emerged into the light blinking and better able to contend with the next downturn. There's been a slow but steady increase in my acceptance of life's messy imperfection, though this could also be defined – in the Buddhist sense – as a *decrease* in the attachment to whatever is happening to me. And from acceptance comes gratitude for life itself: for trees and flowers and mountains and music and birdsong and smells and smiles of people one loves. *Why is there anything at all? Why is there not just nothing?*

Above all I've been relieved not only of the chaos and destruction of active drug addiction but also of the desperate desire for chemical oblivion I thought would never leave me. I haven't needed to 'get out of my head' for years.

• • •

The universe planted usefully sobering reminders in my path. My first clean Christmas found me on the platform of Clapham South station when a couple straight out of Romero's *Dawn of the Dead* – by way of Hogarth's *Rake's Progress* – lurched towards me and proceeded, right there and then, to jab needles into their arms. As the Fall's Mark E. Smith had put it so succinctly, 'no Xmas for John Quays . . .'

When I walked up the Charing Cross Road I saw long-term West End addicts with grey faces and desperate eyes, forever foraging for the next hit. Are any of them still alive? Were they alive *then*? Already it was clear they had opted for death but were hedging their bets by living in the limbo of addiction, their existences revolving around the rituals of scoring and 'clucking' and searching for worn veins in filthy toilets. For a time I'd been able to delude myself that I used drugs to function – to write, to create – but addiction quickly puts the cart before the horse. Ultimately, addicts use in order to use.

The Poor Little Tentacles Of Self

Years later it was strange to be clean and to witness the way addiction was once again being romanticized in pop culture. As the eighties ended it was suddenly cool again to wear leather trousers and black sunglasses; to pose with a Marlboro in the corner of your mouth; to give long interviews about your latest stint in rehab. Rockism, shamed for a decade by designer 'soulcialists' and asexual indie nerds, took its revenge as the mannerisms of seventies hedonists were patched together to make Guns N' Roses and their clones. Even the nerds reinvented themselves as Rolling Stones *redux*: what was Primal Scream's Bobby Gillespie if not Gram Parsons exiled on Main Street?

It was easy to sneer and think 'I saw it all the first time', but this ignored the appeal for an incoming generation that hadn't. In any case, for me to have stopped destroying myself did not alter the eternal symbiosis between music and drugs. By the early nineties it was obvious that even *non*-addicts were getting contact highs from the antics of professional fuck-ups. This coincided neatly with the rise of celebrity culture, whose tacit pact was this: that we allow you to become a Star – to shine in our night sky – but only if you agree to burn out to compensate for our envy. You enact self-destruction in order that we survive.

Ironically, everything I'd written in my self-aggrandizing *NME* piece 'Twilight of the Idols' was true: I could have been inventing Kurt Cobain and

Amy Winehouse in that article. And the truth is that I myself have continued to write about a pantheon of talents whose self-destructiveness was the flipside of their overweening self-regard: Parsons, Arthur Lee, Sly Stone, Montgomery Clift, Tim Hardin, Eddie Hinton, Evan Dando, Elliott Smith, Judee Sill, Karen Dalton, too many more to mention. Does this imply, perhaps, that I remain in thrall to a car-crash narrative of genius, the assumption that talent is a curse born of torment? And is it therefore possible to argue that art itself is a wrestling with restlessness, an effort to fix meaning as the suffering artist is himself fixed by drugs?

Recovery from addiction is relative at best. Few are those who come out the other end of it to testify that self-destruction is not essential to the making of great art. 'There's a notion that artists are kind of impetuous and eccentric and irresponsible and unreliable,' said Tom Waits, a recovering alcoholic himself. 'But I don't think you have to be.' I admire the courage it took for Waits (who'd already written the brilliantly brattish song 'I Don't Wanna Grow Up') to admit he needed to take adult responsibility for his life and his family. Many are the addict friends I've lost along the way because growing up just seemed so, well, uncool. Devo proclaimed in 1981 that they were 'Through Being Cool', but many of us never let go of the posturing that substitutes for a sure sense of Self. Given a choice between being vulnerable and being destructive, addicts routinely opt for the latter. If growing up is only ever a work in progress, admitting to one's immaturity isn't a bad place to start.

• • •

Though I'd renounced the religion of wasted elegance – junked the coolness of junkies – it was harder to forsake my addiction to desire and heartache.

> *Saw RADA production of* Women Beware Women. *Bianca played by beautiful girl whose face made me so uneasy and desperate and sad. Why is it never enough just to behold such beauty? Why this killing need to possess? Perhaps our deepest instinct is to regress to some unconscious bliss. Sexual pleasure is metaphorical. The human body drifts alone: it must attach, interlock.*

If Nietzsche was surely right in *The Gay Science* that the 'wild avarice and injustice of sexual love' has 'furnished the concept of love as the opposite of egoism while it actually may be the most ingenuous expression of [it]', part of me couldn't relinquish the pleasure of wallowing in lovesickness, especially where such immersion was articulated in music.

Nor was I alone in this, for songs of heartbreak bind us all together in a community of the forsaken, and may do something worse: excuse and justify obsession, enshrining love as dependency. ('Most of my songs,' said the late Leonard Cohen, 'are rooted in some kind of inspired confusion of womanhood, godliness, beauty and darkness.') In the way a smell instantly returns us to a specific place and time, so songs evoke emotions attached to failed affairs, plunging us back into the grief we felt. But is this catharsis or merely a refusal to let go?

Songs exist for all points along the arc of doomed love, from early yearnings for someone we can't have to the crushing conclusion that – in Roy Orbison's stark title – 'It's Over'. Any of the following can, if I'm in the right mood, make me cry – or *want* to cry: Little Anthony and the Imperials' 'Goin' Out Of My Head'; the Righteous Brothers 'You've Lost That Lovin' Feelin''; Joy Division's 'Love Will Tear Us Apart'; Elvis Costello's 'I Want You'; Bon Iver's 'Re: Stacks'; the Doobie Brothers' 'What a Fool Believes'; Jimmy Donley's 'Think It Over'; Ben E. King's 'It's All Over'; Soft Cell's 'Say Hello, Wave Goodbye'; Scott Walker's 'On Your Own Again'; Frank Sinatra's 'I'm a Fool to Want You'; Dennis Wilson's 'Thoughts of You'; Nina Simone's 'Little Girl Blue'; Randy Crawford's 'One Day I'll Fly Away'; Todd Rundgren's 'Can We Still Be Friends?'; Kate and Anna McGarrigle's 'Heart Like a Wheel'; George Jones's 'He Stopped Loving Her Today'; Dionne Warwick's 'Anyone Who Had a Heart'; Rickie Lee Jones's 'Company'; Loleatta Holloway's 'Cry to Me'; Bobby Bland's 'Too Far Gone'; Gillian Welch's 'I Made a Lover's Prayer'; Fleetwood Mac's 'Storms'; Carole King's 'Surely'; Jimmy Webb's 'Crying in My Sleep'; Rozetta Johnson's 'Who You Gonna Love'; Dillard & Clark's 'Through the Morning, Through the Night'; Jerry Butler's 'Make It Easy on Yourself'; Alison Krauss's 'New Favorite'; Amy Winehouse's 'Love is a Losing Game'; Two Tons O' Fun's 'Taking Away Your Space'; The Band's 'It Makes No Difference'; Walter Jackson's 'Speak Her Name'; Betty LaVette's 'Let Me Down Easy'; Bettye Swann's 'I'm Just Living a Lie'; Goldfrapp's 'Black Cherry'; Gladys Knight & the Pips' 'Neither One of Us'; Everything But the Girl's 'Missing'; Toto's 'I Won't Hold You Back'; the Shangri-Las' 'Past, Present and Future'; Michael McDonald's 'I Can Let Go Now'; Linda Perhacs' 'Hey, Who Really Cares?'; John Edwards' 'I'll Be Your Puppet'; Rita Wright's 'I Can't Give Back the Love I Feel For You'; Brian Wilson's 'Caroline, No'; the Afghan Whigs' 'I Keep Coming Back'; Kate Bush's 'You're the One'; REO Speedwagon's 'Keep On Loving You'; Sam Dees' 'Worn Out Broken Heart'; Maxayn's 'I Cried My Last Tear'; the Raspberries' 'Starting Over'; Bonnie Raitt's 'I Can't Make You Love Me'; Ron Sexsmith's 'Doomed'; Linda Ronstadt's 'I Never Will Marry'; Sinéad O'Connor's 'Nothing Compares 2 U'; the Blue Nile's 'Family Life'; and Mary J. Blige's 'The Love I Never Had'. Every one of these tracks triggers rich memories of longing and loss, yet I know each of them is an indulgence, a moment plucked from a chocolate box of sorrows.

We come from attachment – from *incorporation*, one might almost say – before our violent ejection from the heaven of unconsciousness that is the womb. We then spend our lives trying to *re*-attach, physically and symbolically, through sex, through family and marriage, status and power, tribal identification. We're all of us alone together, connected yet detached, struggling to bear our separateness.

Like opiate addiction, sexual obsession derives from the need to return to a womblike state – a Motherness – where separation anxiety is assuaged. Unhealthy love is two half-people trying to make a whole, the drama that drives 90 per cent of love songs. But only when I'm whole, integrating the wounded child with the affirming adult, can I give to another: to come and to go, to be close and then to be separate again. Healthy love starts only once the early flush of fixation has faded.

The music of obsession and dependency endures because we remain traumatized by the loss of the original attachment. It endures also because the culture shores up the unhealthiness of obsession. Tabloid celebs flit from one relationship to the next because they need the next thrill of infatuation, the illusion of collapsing into the Other, and thus never experience the deeper joys of fidelity. Monogamy and marriage break down because society worships narcissism and rewards self-gratification.

The Poor Little Tentacles Of Self

Where are the songs of steady, faithful love, the power ballads of lifelong companionship? They don't exist because they don't synch with the attention deficiency demanded by our culture. Music excuses and validates our need to disguise lust as soul-mating, keeping us in perpetual states of longing.

• • •

For some time, living without drugs, I erred on the side of caution, took few risks, lived a regimented and circumscribed life. 'You keep a tight rein on yourself,' Richard observed on emerging from rehab in Chalk Farm.

I was frightened of my own darkness, of whatever inner forces might tip me back into destroying myself. Looking at my journal of the time, I see the handwriting is small, scared, pinched to the point of illegibility. I toned down my prose, narrowing my interests to specialist areas of American roots music. A Birthday Party fan in Australia wrote to say I'd become 'disconcertingly subdued and self-effacing' and wondered what happened in that 'year off' to change me.

Pop culture had in any case become factional and multifarious, *NME* now cheerleading everything and nothing: shiny pop and worthy soul, industrial clanging and South African *mbaqanga*. Under new threat from videos and *Smash Hits* magazine – and from those who'd simply tired of writers name-dropping Barthes in the pages where Julie Burchill and Tony Parsons had once reigned – *NME* lost its monocultural thrust and commenced a long decline only briefly delayed by a flotilla of drippy kids with names like Talulah Gosh and the Shop Assistants.

The paper's tone remained fervently anti-rockist, even when it packed me off to Texas to interview ZZ Top, whose Billy Gibbons turned out to be as erudite as he was facially hirsute – however much it amused him to take this bloodless Brit to 'a high-class titty joint' (his words) where I was embarrassingly lap-danced by a topless and unexpectedly English blonde who struggled to flirt with a man not wearing cowboy boots.

Into the *NME* mix periodically wandered Nick Kent, a ghostly throwback in pungent leather pants that seemed superglued to his long legs. Given that the paper felt no apparent obligation to him and gave him almost no work, it was clear Nick was dropping into the Carnaby Street office simply because he was lonely – and because a few of us were not so fickle as to refuse him the time of day. I even offered help with his opiate problem, but it did not take.

If writing without drugs was hard enough, planning an entire book without them was fraught with fear. Simply overriding the voices in my head that said I could never do it was excruciating. Unaware that perfectionism was only a subtler form of self-loathing, I laboured for months on a proposal. Somehow the research got done and – with my photographer friend Muir – I flew to

America to embark on an epic road trip through Tennessee, Georgia, Alabama, Mississippi and Louisiana, exploring towns where magical music had been made and talking to the soulful hicks who'd made it.

The book got written, though every day of writing began with palpitating panic. Existential determination drove me, self-flagellating whip in hand, to the finishing line. And through the entire process the single most important thing about each day was that I did not put a drug in my body.

Published in 1987, *Say it One Time for the Brokenhearted* was itself a micro-addiction, shutting out anything that was irrelevant to its subject. Perhaps all authors are addicts, obsessive to the point of imbalance. Workaholism is the most insidious of substitute compulsions because it's the hardest to perceive. In our culture, what could possibly be wrong with working too hard? *I cannot spend time with my wife and children because I'm working so hard to better their lives.* Life itself is endlessly deferred, the plateau I never reach.

Perhaps writing is obsessive because it's a luxury. Art is egomaniacal because the artist presumes he has more important things to say than his fellows do. But many people are more eloquent in their daily speech than their self-regarding friends are on the page. I know I write because, neurotically, I wish to leave something behind. Perhaps that way I can cheat death. Vanity of vanities, all is vanity . . .

My own workaholism may not have had the hazardous consequences heroin and cocaine addiction had for me – or that sex or gambling addictions have for others – but it's removed me from life in the broadest sense of that word: kept me from intimacy with others, sons and lovers and friends alike; kept me in my own head and unwilling to plunge into the spontaneous experience of the everyday. 'For a guy like me, the work is always the last thing to go,' the late *New York Times* reporter David Carr wrote in his addiction memoir *The Night of the Gun*. 'It is, in some twisted way, more sacred, more worthy of protection, than friends, loved ones, and family.'

I've been back in that state of feverish busy-ness and wild rage about money, and have come to the unhappy conclusion that I must actually be addicted to this state of mind. I see with blinding clarity that I'm terrified of losing control of my life – that everything I do is about ensuring things don't get away from me. I am so neurotic and untrusting. I tell myself I have some theoretical faith in a higher power, a greater being, but in fact I have almost none.

Unlike heroin – or poker, or prostitutes – work is not something I can abstain from, but nor should it be something I use to hide from life. At what point do I say: I have proved myself, done enough to stop and take it all in? But we live in a time that honours Doing rather than Being, when ceaseless achievement is the principal measure of worth and most of us succumb to what Vaclav Havel called 'the world of things, surfaces, frantic consumption and self-absorption'.

Western society is itself addictive, compulsive and obsessively materialist. I've been seduced into unmanageable debt so I can have nice things and keep up with my neighbours. I put quantifiable Matter before unquantifiable Spirit, forgetting that the happiest moments are almost always free. If I could stop myself buying into the gloom of the daily headlines, I might learn again that less is more, and that there's greater pleasure to be gained from roaming in the park than from turning my kids into shopaholic mall rats.

Capitalism fooled us into believing it's amusing to own a hundred pairs of Jimmy Choos, but when is enough enough? Answer: never, if you're trying to fill the hole in your soul with a pair of ankle-crippling stilettos. Some people are so poor, all they have is money. One day we'll look back and wonder how human beings became so hollow and so shallow.

• • •

I've tried stuffing the hole with sex, money, clothes, cars – anything material or abstractly symbolic (power,

Montréal, April 2016

prestige, status, etc.) – but there's only one thing that actually fills it. Call it what you will, but I have slowly and reluctantly accepted the word God as a synonym for the vibrating, super-strung *Is-ness* of the known and unknowable universe.

For all the evil that distorts and warps religious belief, the absence of any belief at all may be more worrying still. If 'God' is to mean anything, it must mean everything and nothing, without gender, race or face, as vast and colour-less as the wind. 'Religions,' John Gray wrote in *Black Mass*, 'are not claims to knowledge but ways of living with what cannot be known.'

Some contend that all addicts are searching for God, for spiritual wholeness and connection, finding it fleetingly in a chemical intoxication that relieves the pressures of the ego. M. Scott Peck went so far as to describe addiction as 'the sacred disease'. Certainly I would suggest that any addict who does not replace the relieving power of narcotics with the power of spiritual connection is doomed to fall back into chemical abuse.

I cannot exactly say what Spirit is, unless it's a right-brain metaphor for everything not bluntly material and left-brain-measurable: the counterpoint to the ego's self-centred terror. For all my distaste at hearing the word 'God' spat from the mouths of fundamentalists, I have as big a problem with materialists who reduce sentient life to selfish genetics and seek to expose altruism as a disingenuous fiction.

'Find yourself, forgive yourself, forget yourself': this was how I once heard a fellow traveller summarize the journey out of addiction. It's a perfect paradox that I can only forgive and forget the Self once I've found it. 'Know thyself,' exhorted the ancient Greeks, who also counselled that we should do 'nothing in excess'. Both those formulae lodged themselves in my memory when I heard them in a classroom at thirteen. Neither saved me from the addiction that lay ahead; both have assisted in ongoing abstinence and recovery. When I stopped taking drugs at twenty-four I knew next to nothing about myself. I'd told myself so many lies about who I was and what I felt. I was advised that if I could be honest and present myself to the world as I was – in groups and in one-to-one communication – things would work out. If, on the other hand, I wore a mask and people liked it, I would never know if they liked me or liked the mask.

• • •

Six years after getting clean, with my first son born, I saw that I'd always tried to stay one step ahead of my damage, terrified to turn and face it. Denying to myself that there were deep disturbances which reared up in bursts of uncontainable rage, I was attempting, futilely, to evade my hard-wired emotional conditioning – to avoid and ultimately disown myself. I was running from the truth of the past as it lived and breathed in me, yet the inner turmoil kept nipping at my heels and insisting there were 'issues' to be dealt with.

One day, determined that my son should not be frightened of his father, I turned for the first time to face the monster at my back, only to realize it was the phantom of my own unlovability, an ingrained shame I couldn't shift without help.

'Anger is an energy,' Johnny Rotten had snarled on PiL's 'Rise'. And he was right: the cauterizing rage of punk was a necessary purging of rock's pomposity. Yet anger in this world has surely done more bad than good. From local quarrels to global conflicts, anger seems to beget only more anger, endless eye-for-an-eye revenge and retaliation. And perhaps it will and must always be like that: Utopian efforts to pre-empt conflict are invariably good intentions that pave roads to greater hells.

Still, I suspect that unacknowledged personal rage is what ultimately fuels all ideological strife. The belief that I must get my way or else be reckoned a failure causes more misery than any other I subscribe to. 'We will cease to be so angry once we cease to be so hopeful,' suggested Seneca, who centuries ago saw the world for the intransigent force it is. Better to have no expectations and simply accept the way life unfolds.

What *really* makes us angry, however, is the store of undeclared hurt we lug around, the disowned pain of childhood neglect and abuse. I cannot proceed with the present because I'm forever dealing with unfinished business. Furthermore, I'm constantly ready to react or attack as a way of discharging buried rage. Prison psychiatrist James Gilligan has suggested that 'all violence is an attempt to replace shame with self-esteem'.

Anger is a hot brick passed from one human to another. It says that if I can dump my feelings in a kind of misguided catharsis, I won't have them anymore. Now *you* will have them, until you in turn dump them on the next innocent bystander. The healthy human rejects the brick, but most of us are so wounded at our core that we accept the other's anger in the unconscious belief we deserve it.

I'd go still further: the man who seeks to dump his anger on another – in a road-rage incident, for instance – seldom selects a secure person as his target. His antennae instinctively identify the person who'll lock horns with him and enable the supposedly cathartic explosion to occur. But the catharsis never does occur, since it's always followed by shame that only fuels further rage.

My wife once told me the instructive story of a woman who was being aggressively rude at a party but who, on being asked if she was okay, burst into tears. Sometimes I think all human communication is a game of rocks, paper and scissors: either we meet each other head-on – symmetrically, as Bateson would have put it – or we try to complement each other, to respond in ways that enfold the other's pathology.

One of the best advertising slogans I've ever seen on a billboard is 'You Are Not Stuck in Traffic. You Are Traffic'. For road rage is predicated on a belief – a symmetrical one – that I'm separate from the traffic, that it's Me and My Car versus all other drivers in *their* cars. This is the atomized state of the individual hitting the intolerable brick wall of the fact that s/he must share the world with others. I offer it merely as a metaphor for the frustration of the ego that believes its agenda should trump everybody else's: a chronic impatience born of a desperate need to *get there* because being stuck in traffic for even a minute is an unbearable obligation to sit with one's own feelings.

The driver at peace with himself – or with his past as it manifests in the moment – goes with the (non-)flow. He knows there's nothing he can do but submit to it. Drive through central London or Paris or Manhattan for a day and you'll encounter thousands of drivers who act like sharks, apparently believing that if they stop they will die. They cannot accept, or do not know, that they are part of the totality of humanity as it takes the temporary form of that traffic.

To return to the source of rage is essential for the recovering addict. Through years of groups and therapy I've come not just to understand the pain at my core but to feel it and accept it – and even to release some of it. Not having the option of self-medication, I have to confront the emptiness at the heart of me, bear the awareness of it and allow others to fill it with love to the point where I can love myself. I have to stop avoiding the void.

The most heartbreaking people in the world are the abused boys and girls of whom Camilla Batmanghelidjh said that 'getting them to feel love is the most painful thing you can do, and the hardest thing for them to bear'. For these children it may never be possible to trust another human being, so betrayed have they been by those who should have cared for them – who almost certainly in turn suffered the lovelessness that's handed down from generation to generation.

How easy it would have been never to know that I was lovable, that I deserved joy. How close I came at twenty-four to ending my life because I could no longer stand to be inside my mind. How I despised my own face and body, how ashamed I felt of almost everything I did and said. How long it took to start loving myself as the imperfect and ridiculous creature I am.

But how worth the wait it was.

• • •

What is most frightening for the addict is the very freedom he thinks he is searching for: the freedom of the choices life offers when he is really open to it. If addiction is usually an impatient shortcut to spiritual fulfilment – a kind of cheat – it is *always* a fearful contraction of life in its vast diversity: a freedom *from* choice rather than *of* it. The addict released from prison is thrust back into a world of alarming possibilities, asked once again to be responsible for his actions and decisions. What to do first, what to do next: where to go when – for months or for years – every step has been predetermined.

As dangerous as prison can be, inmates have told me they feel safer within its walls than outside them. Not because there aren't scary people inside them – wardens and fellow prisoners alike – but because there's nothing quite as frightening as being pushed back into the infinite existential void of the world.

Wherever I go, there I am.

Given that addiction itself is a kind of elective prison,

it's hardly surprising that addicts return to the rituals that put them behind bars in the first place. Prison is society's containment of its most transparent pain and dysfunction yet does little or nothing to make prisoners less dependent. Among the most moving experiences of my life have been visits to prisons to talk of my own addiction, walking into rooms of shutdown men whose fronts slowly melt as I – in my apologetically over-privileged way – try to speak honestly of self-hatred and 'dis-ease'. To watch these angry men become vulnerable boys is a privilege so rare it makes you weep as you take your leave of them.

The postscript is that the very people you thought would make it are often the ones who come out and, within a week of release, overdose and die.

It's another beautiful Saturday, but death is never far away. Felix, a sweet gentle Kiwi who made tea at our group, OD'd last weekend. I don't know what to feel other than a numb despair.

Somewhere along the line you become inured to such loss. Phrases like 'What a waste' sound hollow after you've said them a hundred times. In my memory I summon a string of people I tried to help: men and women dead at twenty-seven, thirty-three, forty-six, sixty-seven years old. Did they use again because they thought, 'I can get away with it for a night'? Or did they say to themselves, 'I don't give a fuck any more'?

Never Enough

I hear addicts personify their addiction – 'the disease wants me dead' – as if the suicidal impulse comes somehow from without. But every addict must acknowledge his own death wish. Depressive feelings of worthlessness are a constant accompaniment to spiritual growth, for life continually disappoints us. Resentment against those who do not reward me – or do not even think of me – is the rageful trigger for most relapses. Gradually accepting I will never matter as much to others as I do to myself is the toughest lesson I have to learn in this life. I've wasted too much time hurting at perceived injustice while taking for granted the good fortune that comes my way. Why? Because enough is never enough: no sooner is the addict fed than he is hungry again, craving something to fill the hole where love should be.

To expect nothing is the only freedom; otherwise I'm forever awaiting the email or phone call that will make things complete. That place, that plateau where all will at last be well: *I never get there*. Yet I spend my life chasing the mirage, deferring happiness as I gaze enviously at others who've apparently arrived at this Shangri-La. Though they may wish one to think otherwise, they aren't there yet either.

The *Chuang Tzu* urges me to stop struggling in the water, to let the current take me where it will. Many times I've thought I was about to drown, yet I have stayed afloat. I do not get what I want in this world. Often I do not even get what I need. I get what I get, and I either roll with it or condemn myself to perpetual misery.

• • •

Over the course of twenty clean years I fell for a handful of women who – in the popular phrase – were 'unavailable'. Well-meaning friends pointed out a pattern, suggesting it was safer to fall for and fantasize about people I could not have. By the same token, the women I did date were those I intuitively knew could not hurt me. Did my pathology therefore doom me to desire only those who *could*? Was the unavailability itself the erotic charge? And was I returning obsessively to some *ur-abandonment* in a vain effort to rewrite my history?

Worse still was the possibility that I unconsciously set these women up to reject me: the elegant French-Canadian in the black pants-suit with whom I dreamily danced to Grace Jones's 'La Vie en Rose' at Muir's party in Notting Hill – and who pressed her pretty lips to mine in a taxi but turned out, after three dinners, to have a boyfriend back in Montréal; the German with the piercing green eyes who worked for a top pop star of the day and blew hot and cold before accusing me of being a 'Mimosa' (a plant whose characteristics I had to look up in a horticultural dictionary).

I float through the Age of Chivalry exhibition at the Royal Academy and feel only a sickening dread in my stomach – the thought of K. There is something fatale *about this fraulein with the mesmerizing eyes and Giaconda smile. Will I ever want another kind of girl? Does it have to be like this and is one supposed to enjoy it? I must be an abject wretch to be so consumed with desire. I should turn this around and think, 'No, I am getting on with my life and will not be suspended on this point of longing for someone I hardly know.' If I could only stop wondering if the phone is about to ring . . .*

These girls were not Sara but their pull sucked me once again into obsession. 'This sickness keeps me wanting,' Green Gartside sighed on Scritti Politti's delectable 'A Little Knowledge', which soundtracked what he oxy-moronically described to me as 'sweetly sad pleasure'. My sense of self remained so porous that I simply wished to collapse into female beauty. If I was at least risking hurt and not anaesthetizing it, the prospect of rejection remained life-threatening. And the *mädchen* was right: I *was* a Mimosa, or at least a man who, seized by desire, did not care enough for himself to simulate dignity.

How I detest being at the mercy of a woman's whims. The uncertainty, the risk of pain . . . it's intolerable. I wish I had the strength to forget about her. The scared boy simply refuses to be hurt and humiliated again.

The concept of love addiction took root at this time: we learned of Women Who Love Too Much and of their male counterparts. Today it's acknowledged as a destructive compulsion like any other. My sister, who works in the addiction field, told me – long before Steve McQueen's film *Shame* – that the bleakest souls she counsels are sex addicts, men and women who use each other's bodies like deadened automatons and act out pantomimes of intimacy that mask their inability to connect. The ritual of seduction – the enactment of desire – is everything, the dearth of emotional care exposed the minute the act is completed. For all the feverish coupling, the gleeful self-abasement, everything has been taking place in the addict's head, where fantasy can be controlled.

I have done my share of disconnected sex. I also believe that eroticism was pornographized for me at an early age and that I've never fully undone the yoking of desire to exploitation and exhibitionism. If Updike was right when he stated – with almost piercing innocence – that 'a naked woman is, for most men, the most beautiful thing they will ever see', why then has male desire become so furtive, so shameful?

The belief is that if I don't get laid I will die: sex represents some impossible union – the suspension of time in which all will be healed and I will be made whole. X's body holds a promise of blissful suspension, even when I don't particularly like her.

113

*The idea of getting a girl into bed is really no differ-
ent from the idea of shooting a snowball. I think it's
going to stop time and fix me, even when I know it
won't and there will be hell – deeper isolation and
alienation – to follow.*

If there's a difference between sex addiction and love
addiction, it may only be a matter of volume. The sex
addict seeks multiple consecutive partners in the desperate quest for relief from Self. The love addict – or serial
monogamist – pours his energies into the one *obscur objet
du désir* with the same goal in view. Both return continually to the same place of fear, unable to be friends to
themselves. In the forlorn credo of Carl Dreyer's Gertrud:
'I believe in the pleasures of the flesh and the irreparable
loneliness of the soul.'

• • •

While the toughest feelings I've had to bear in recovery
have inevitably involved unrequited desire, the most painful time in the last thirty years was the slow death of my
first marriage and the dissolution of the family I'd helped
to create. It may not have been coincidental that the marriage started to die at a time when the family was living in
upstate New York and I was immersed in work to the point
of neglecting not only them but the recovery that had made
it possible to be a husband and father in the first place.

'The loneliness of the soul': Carl Dreyer's *Gertrud*
(Palladium/REX/Shutterstock)

For the better part of four years I made do with the bare minimum of one group a week, usually slouching at the back of a church hall and only rarely opening my mouth. I told myself I felt too different from these

Americans, but the decision to remain on the periphery of recovery was a choice I'd unconsciously made not to share myself with others. I didn't want to use drugs in this time but I did not grow emotionally or spiritually. Certainly I grew away from my wife.

When we made the decision to return to England in 1999, she went back ahead to supervise work on the Clapham house where I'd used so many drugs and suffered so long over Sara. The first phone call she made from London was enough to tell me the marriage was over. There was a chilly efficiency in her voice that spelled the end of any love we still had for each other.

The grief for a broken marriage – for a family cleaved in two – does not end, even when it abates. It's a wound that never quite heals, and to this day I feel it as a failure for my children and as the trauma it was in their young lives. Nor will I forget the stark moment of realization as I sat on the edge of the marital bed one night: my marriage is over and I will have to find another home; please say I am going to wake from this nightmare.

As it turned out, my children survived and flourished. Moreover, the divorce was the making of me, the vital next stage in my growing up. I found out who I was and what I wanted, not least because I recommitted to recovery and began attending a men's group I'd always shunned. The members of this group have been my brothers now for over fifteen years and shared my

116

struggles at every turn, as I've shared theirs. For me the group – like others I regularly attend – is the best show in town, a transformative coming-together of males of all ages and backgrounds, in this specific case without the irresistible distraction of women for whom we'd otherwise tailor what we reveal. These men are my true peers, the friends I 'get' and who get me. I cannot conceive of life without them.

If ultimately we're alone in our own heads, infinitely remote from each other, we get to share our separateness if we choose. That makes all the difference between harrowing loneliness and bearable solitude.

• • •

After my marriage ended I found myself once again besotted by the woman – the Sara-substitute – I'd loved almost twenty years before. I was unprepared for how engulfing the feelings would be, how deep the longing would feel for what I could not have.

> *I have to believe these feelings are not about her anyway: I could cathect on to anyone right now. I'm just a ball of need, which she probably gleans anyway. Why can't I look after myself for a moment? Why is it so unbearable just to be (with) me?*

For the better part of three years, while she stayed married and I dated other women, I thought and dreamed of her and lived for our infrequent encounters.

I saw her last night and felt what I always feel: her beauty breaks my heart. Some cosmic prankster had sat me beside her, with a setup blonde to my left, so I had the dear girl to myself for the best part of an hour. Is romantic infatuation merely the dread of loss and death? You want someone so badly that the prospect of them withdrawing is an annihilation.

I lurched from ecstasy to numb demoralization and back again. I made more tapes of heartbreak songs (Lewis Taylor's 'Satisfied', Beck's 'Lonesome Tears') and drove through London playing them, smiling with tears in my eyes. 'The soul apparently needs amorous sadness,' noted Thomas Moore, who knew there was something sweet in the feelings that coalesce around romantic agony. Music wants us to wallow in pain, to hear lovesickness framed in heartbreaking phrases. It's not just a vehicle for catharsis but a universal language of identification: *I'm not the only one who ever felt this abandoned.*

Slowly I found the strength to cease subjecting myself to such torment, forcing myself to look elsewhere again. But it took a brusque Scottish therapist to empty a bucket of cold Highlands water on my fantasies: 'She's married. It's not an option.' I was a child in need of firm boundaries.

The Poor Little Tentacles Of Self

I was in my mid-forties – and divorced for three years – by the time I was ready for a relationship where passion and playfulness were matched by equality and respect. It took that long to grow into a man who could share his life with a real woman.

Within minutes of meeting my future wife I knew it would be easy between us. She was as lovely as she looked, her beauty an emblem of her spirit and not a mask. Yet it was not easy to trust: for a long time I suffered at the thought that a more natural match for her would be the dark stranger of romantic folklore, a dashing cad with designer stubble and designs on spiriting her away. 'The *odiosamato* (as the Italians call the "rival") is *also* loved by me,' Barthes had written brilliantly in his *Lover's Discourse*: 'he interests me, intrigues me, appeals to me.'

Am afflicted by the deep dread that N. will forsake me for the demon Don Juan who steals beauties from their faithful lovers. Being in this state of adoration activates ancient memories of S. and stirs fears that N. might toy with me. I'm trying to believe I can give in to this consuming desire without it taking over my life.

I'd fallen for a Yorkshire lass who looked more like a California girl in her designer jeans and bangles. Friends assumed I'd tumbled only for the outside form, but we were the same age and at the same place in our lives, over and through divorces with sons of roughly parallel ages. She was from a different world but had listened to Bolan and Bowie in Barnby Dun as I was hearing them in Battersea.

I tried hard not to play lovers' games but was insecure enough to feel deep fear – encroaching abandonment – if I did not hear from her at pre-agreed times.

Why do I have to ache for her when she's gone? But isn't that what I wanted – to feel this passionately? I sit at the computer trying to focus on work and words, but flowing under everything is the current of my need, the throb of my love. The silence is so loud and I'm so alone in it.

Often I rehearsed for a betrayal I thought I could not survive.

Is there nothing between loving helplessly and wanting to run? Am I panicked because I'm so close to the love I've always sought? Or is this just addiction – to her lips and her skin and the smell of her? It doesn't matter how much I process it, I feel like a child torn from the breast. I want to punish her for the fact that I love her.

Eventually my addictive need calmed down and I was simply able to be myself. 'I can't imagine a more lonely person down deep,' said a friend of the great L.A. crime writer Ross MacDonald; 'looking for the person whom he could freely and without concentration be with, somebody who didn't constantly keep him in a state of self-definition . . .' For her I did not need to pretend to be anything other than what I am. I was finally known and loved as the vain, foolish, but essentially decent man I know myself to be. I think this is what people refer to as 'intimacy'.

What joy to be walking about Manhattan, hand in hand with someone who makes your heart glad, who isn't tricky, who's honest and direct, who loves you as much as you love her . . .

The trust – the deep commitment we've made to each other – is the sexiest thing that's ever happened to me. I've watched couples destroy each other in the name of love, when loving was the last thing they were doing to each other. 'A healthy relationship,' my Scottish therapist had said, 'is one in which each person is able to walk away from the other. Anything else is a dependency.'

Naturally I have my dependencies on her, as she does on me. But they're small ones: I believe we are two whole people who'd flourish alone but choose to walk our way together.

On Hudson Street, in a room full of women talking about men, I heard that a healthy relationship should be 'present, mutual and equal', and that when it's right you should 'a) listen to her, b) light up when she enters the room, and c) have no plans for her improvement'.

More critical than anything has been the willingness to work through difference and conflict, to tell uncomfortable truths when they are required – 'to go into the muddle', as my great friend Paul puts it. It would be strange if we hadn't had watershed moments of extreme divergence – when care and compassion took backseats to our egos – but neither of us has ever seriously believed the end was nigh. I've been typically male in my grumpy selfishness, she's been typically female in her desire to make things perfect. Yet we feel secure in the teamwork we have to do. We share enough passions and enjoy doing enough things separately.

Addicts in couple relationships are prone to bouts of destructive self-sabotage, preferring them to frustration and vulnerability – which are mostly what life consists of. Underpinning everything in such relationships must be the commitment to keep trying, laughing, apologizing; to compromise; to speak honestly without blaming or abusing; to keep growing together, never taking the other for granted or seeking to change her into something s/he is not.

How does one keep romantic love new? By knowing that each unfolding moment is itself new, that only the ego's perception makes the familiar seem stale. We reinvent our relationships in every second we spend with each other. If things feel predictable we try to let some light in, expose the relationship to fresh input. We make the effort to extend ourselves into the world, to see beyond the ends of our own noses and see our partners as they actually are. 'Everybody wants it to be summer all the time, in relationships and with their career,' Tom Waits has said. 'When the weather starts to turn, they think they'd better get out. So it takes a certain amount of persistence.'

It's hard to write of calm and contentedness, since so often they seem to be the ends or resolutions of stories about pain and torment. Yet if literature conspires against happiness, there's a duty to speak of ease and quiet joy. If it sounds smug or bland, it's meant only to suggest that we're not doomed to stay in pain and dysfunction – that even if the ego continually reasserts its hold we can slowly evolve into giving spirits and let go of the need to impose Self on Other. We cannot banish the ego but we can notice its insidious invasions. We can move beyond Self simply by becoming aware of the ego's insatiability.

• • •

When recovering addicts speak of Self – in the contexts of 'self-worth', 'self-loathing', 'self-obsession', etc. – we are essentially referring to a problematic narcissism. Lacking core experience of being loved and held as children, we ceaselessly seek consolation for that lack. Without drugs, substitute addictions rush to the rescue and temporarily deflect us from the central problem of Self. In recovery I seesaw between self-aggrandizement and self-hatred, lord of all I survey or the lowest beggar in the gutter.

Saw afresh that my moods broadly follow a bipolar trajectory: I'm either 'up' (approved of) or 'down' (threatened or nullified in some way) – and the slightest thing can tip me one way or the other. There seems to be nothing between terror and omnipotence: I'm either stewing in self-doubt or cruising on the ego's superhighway. I am almost never just 'okay'.

If there seems to be no third way, it's because I've never truly accepted myself as the flawed and comical being I am. I simply take myself – and life itself – too seriously. 'When you let it, life can be so heavy,' said the singer Robert Wyatt. 'Gravity becomes too great, and you can hardly function. And I think the thing is to somehow become a kind of gas and float above it.'

I've never heard a spiritual position expressed quite like this – especially by a professed Marxist – but I think it's what Wyatt was doing when he said it. The Self strives neurotically to become separate and solid, as if only that will prove its worth to others. But the separate self is an illusion, a materialist construct. A healthy subjectivity is the awareness of that illusion and a consequent embracing of as much Otherness as the ego will permit. Only when I come to terms with what I am (and am not) can I begin to bear the fact that I do not matter.

Let me qualify that. I matter to those I'm responsible for: my dependants require me to provide food, shelter, clothing. Beyond that, I matter only insofar as my vanity – or at least my dread of death – compels me to attract attention. 'Once a person isn't hungry,' Jaron Lanier wrote in *You Are Not a Gadget*, 'a desire for status can become as intense as the earlier quest for food.' This desire sits at the root of all my anxiety, exacerbated now by social media and the need to stand out from the crowd. There's such a desperate hunger to be somebody and mean something – or just to be heard above all the techno-babble – that I lose sight of the paradox that meaning is only attained by pulling back into solitariness. Many cultural pundits have pronounced on this melancholy theme in the past decade. Never before in history have intellectuals been so worried that the interior life of the mind is disappearing.

For the addict of the twenty-first century, the challenge to recover and heal is made doubly difficult by the fact that the whole of society – and the entire machine of global capitalism – has become addictive and compulsive. None of us is enough; we all need to be bigger, better, richer. I strive to possess material things for the simple reason that I cannot possess spirit, yet power, wealth and status will always be shabby substitutes for the love I secretly crave.

'It is not the I . . . that is given up,' Martin Buber wrote in words that echo Robert Wyatt's, 'but that false self-asserting instinct that makes a man flee to the possessing of things before the unreliable, perilous world of relation which has neither density nor duration and cannot be surveyed.' That 'world of relation' is the universe as it actually is, a space of chaos my ego cannot shape to its own ends, a vastness in which the 'We' is paramount and the 'I' negligible. True peace stems from acceptance of powerlessness over vastness, the humility of knowing how small I am and how little difference I make. 'Why can't she get that . . . she is clinging to crooked beliefs because she so fears the alternative,' Irving Yalom wrote of a patient in his *Momma and the Meaning of Life*; 'that she lives in a universe absolutely indifferent to whether she is happy or unhappy?'

Chekhov intimated as much in his beloved story 'Lady with Lapdog', suggesting that in the sea's 'complete indifference to the life and death of each one of us' was paradoxically hidden 'the guarantee of our eternal salvation'.

● ● ●

Could one ever claim one was 'cured' of the condition of addiction? I give only one answer to those who say to me, intermittently, 'Come on, after all this time, surely one drink . . .' And that is: 'It's not something I care to put to the test.'

True, I can't be absolutely certain that taking the first drug – the first pill, the first glug of gin – will condemn me once more to chronic addiction. But here's the rub: *I cannot be sure it won't.* Too many test themselves after years of abstinence, only to plunge back into the daily hell of scoring and withdrawing. Too many do not make it back alive.

Do I ever *want* to use? I can reach the end of a taxing day and think, *Hmmm, a stiff whisky would take the edge off this stress.* I can enter a room-full of strangers at a party and think, fleetingly, *These lucky bastards don't have to endure their shyness and awkwardness as I do.* But these are the most evanescent of thoughts. If a drink were the only way to decompress or to ease tension, how sad an indictment of the human spirit that would be. Once I accepted the door to drugs was padlocked shut, I didn't greatly miss them. If the door remains even fractionally ajar, the addict will eventually walk through it.

Life never stops obstructing, never stops lobbing span-ners into the works. My father once said, with a wise smile, that life was 'just one damned thing after another'. It is, but I can be a victim of it or I can detach and know that I'm more than what is happening to me. The mys-tics tell me I have a still centre that survives all trials, even the approach of death. I'm not defined by what I do or what I own; I'm defined only by my presence and my consciousness in these flowing moments. 'Things will happen which will trample and pierce,' wrote the poet Edward Thomas, 'but I shall go on, something that is here and there like the wind, something unconquerable, something not to be separated from the dark earth and the light sky, a strong citizen of infinity and eternity.'

Had I attempted to solve the riddle of my addiction using my own cerebellum I'd be dead today or worse: one of the *living* dead stumbling and sleepwalking through a numbed world of Not Feeling. (Feelings do not kill, it turns out, but it can feel as if they're about to.) I've shared my journey through feelings with thousands of kindred spirits – some who bailed before the miracle happened, many still in my life after three decades. Abstinence may not guarantee sanity but it gives me a chance of changing into a person I can stand – and even, one fine day, love.

• • •

When people ask me if drugs should be legalized, usually my answer is: 'I don't know.' Broadly I accept that the War on Drugs has been hopelessly counter-productive – or worse, as Eugene Jarecki's harrowing 2012 film *The House I Live In* suggested. (Far from America's war being a failure, it turns out to have been a huge success, creating a boom industry in persecution and incarceration.) Jarecki traced the roots of said 'war' back to attacks on opium-smoking Chinese immigrants in the nineteenth century, but the cynicism of Richard Nixon's backtracking on the need for drug treatment in favour of election-winning bellicosity towards 'peddlers' was no less contemptible. Every politician from Nixon to Clinton has colluded with the lie of the drug 'menace'.

At the same time I wonder whether I, and others like me, would be alive today if I'd been able to use heroin and cocaine with impunity. Even if one accepts that Prohibition in 1930s America was futile, does the legal use of alcohol not arguably do more harm than good? And why in any case has alcohol – a drug far more destructive than most criminalized substances – been singled out for legal use?

• • •

It's difficult not to despair at the state of the world we hear and read about each day, to all but give up on what J. G. Ballard defined as 'the human family, a primate species with an unbelievable appetite for cruelty and violence'. Like most people, I assume, I feel this despair each morning as I read the paper and listen to the radio. The world is simultaneously magical and diabolical, and it's tough to keep the two things juxtaposed. In *The Warmth of the Heart Prevents Your Body from Rusting*, Marie de Hennezel quotes one Abbé Pierre, who counsels us to keep both eyes open on life: one on its suffering, the other on its wondrous beauty.

I'm not sure I ever felt more despair about the human race than when I read of the Holocaust survivor who – after Hezbollah launched rockets into Israel in 2006 – insisted 'we should kill [them] like flies'. At that moment I thought, 'What if George Santayana was only half-right? What if even those who *aren't* ignorant of the past are condemned to repeat it?'

Yet what if people – *groups* above all – simply need things to hate? What if humanity only evolves through identifying abstractions known as 'them'? Decades after Auschwitz and Treblinka, the genocidal strain is alive and thriving in the human psyche, as is the simple need to demonize 'the Other' as the embodiment of all that's wrong. When the designer John Galliano's 'loss of control' in a bar in the Marais led to his outbursts of anti-Semitism and Islamophobia, his *fashionista* pals rallied round to protest how out of character his abuse was, as if drugs had somehow infected him with anti-Semitism and Islamophobia. What no one dared say was that addiction is so often allied to resentment: the entrenched belief that my unhappiness is your fault.

As a schoolboy I was shown documentaries about Nazi concentration camps, the almost incredible images of which I've never been able to erase from memory. Surely, I think to myself now, any child exposed to such images can only be, for want of a better term, pro-Semitic. But the Jews of Europe were very precisely seen as *not human*, subhuman at best. They were darkness incarnate, essence of otherness.

Is there not a way we could bequeath our children a set of universal principles that made such dehumanization impossible? Or must we accept that demonization – the collective projection of our dark messy shit on to others – is woven into the very fabric of 'civilization'? In *People of the Lie*, M. Scott Peck defined evil as 'the use of power to destroy the spiritual growth of others for the purpose of defending and preserving the integrity of our own sick selves'. At a micro level, this is what happens in the playground or on social media; at the macro level it's what happened in Nazi Germany, in Bosnia, in Rwanda – and what may yet happen in Trump's America, Le Pen's France, and elsewhere in a world that's lurching back to fascism. But what's even more interesting is to watch how it happens in one's own life.

For a long time I struggled to contain feelings of intolerance towards an acquaintance whose perceived irresponsibility and selfishness enraged me. The fact that much of his behaviour exemplified little more than a carefree hedonism did not change my unacknowledged dislike of his freedom to do as he pleased. It did not seem fair that I, who'd striven for so long to be good, should have to tolerate someone concerned mainly with his own pleasure. Inevitably it was the wee therapist who first floated the dreaded 'E' word past me. Envy, as I at least knew theoretically, was the engine of most discontent in the world, but feeling it for my friend surely made me a bad person.

Little shifted for me until, in a sincere effort to get to the bottom of it, I unburdened myself to my lifelong pal Christian. Invoking Jung, he suggested I properly own the part of myself that longed to be irresponsible. By trying for so long to be good, and by being so rigorous and inflexible in that virtuousness, I had split off into shaming, self-righteous destructiveness towards anyone who'd apparently got away with not growing up. My internalized, shaming Parent – mother and father conjoined – thus punished my Inner Child.

Something switched in me in that moment: not completely or irreversibly, but profoundly nonetheless. 'Lighten up' was one lesson, but also: 'Be a bit bad. Let Pan come out to play'. Foregoing alcohol and narcotics did not mean I had to be a (self-)punishing Puritan. The friend can still aggravate me, but I no longer deny that I sometimes long to cram myself full of ice cream and not tidy the bedroom. I also make the oblique connection between my desire to scapegoat him and the demonization that leads to persecution. Under the right circumstances, the most virtuous of us are capable of the most appalling cruelty.

• • •

The Poor Little Tentacles Of Self

On 21 August 2003, Ian MacDonald – possibly the best British popular music writer of his generation – emailed me to check some rather pedestrian fact whose import is now lost to time. The following day he killed himself.

I've often wondered to myself: 'Ian, if you were so close to ending your life on Wednesday, how could that fact have mattered to you so much on Tuesday?' Not to mention: 'Was there something I should've read between those lines that might have given a clue to your state of mind?'

Though I no longer have Ian's email, I'm sure the answer to the latter question is No. It's entirely likely that, on Tuesday 22 August, Ian had no plan to kill himself the following day (which would be the answer to the previous question). Just where the tipping-point lies that pushes a man to end his life must remain a mystery to all who knew him, even those who knew he was unhappy. I'm awed by that moment of enactment, the choice to turn out the light forever. How shockingly alone you must feel in the instant of stepping into eternal night.

I hardly knew Ian – never met him, had only the most perfunctory of dealings with him – but was affected enough by his writing to attend his funeral, along with several of the *NME* veterans who'd worked with him in the paper's glory years. When tall Tony Tyler, in the eulogy, read a line from Ian's last letter to his parents – 'My loneliness was acute and caused me great misery' – I felt a heartrending sadness for a man whose writing had been so full of compassion and wisdom. 'Can it be,' he'd written in an extraordinary essay on his fellow suicide (and Cambridge contemporary) Nick Drake, 'that the materialist worldview, in which there is no intrinsic meaning, is slowly murdering our souls?'

How could the man who wrote the sublime pieces in *The People's Music*, published shortly before his death, take his own life? But then how could the American writer David Foster Wallace kill himself after writing that 'if you've really learned how to think, how to pay attention . . . it will be within your power to experience a crowded, loud, slow, consumer-hell-type situation as not only meaningful but sacred, on fire with the same force that lit the stars – compassion, love, the sub-surface unity of all things'?

Why did Vic Chesnutt kill himself – on Christmas Day of all days – after admitting that 'I am always at extremes. Maybe that's what powers me. I can go from "I'm a lover" to "I'm despicable, toxic trash". When I remember there's a whole giant universe out there, then I feel good'?

Why did Elliott Smith, horrifically, stab himself to death after writing some of the subtlest songs of the past two decades and profoundly touching a mass of fans with the quiet fire of his self-examination?

How was it that the insight of these men – with all the self-knowledge in the world, one might say – was powerless against their deep urge to obliterate the hated, humiliated parts of their psyches?

The answer is right there in my own experience, for I have myself gone from rapturous happiness to hopeless despair, and from there to the beckoning fantasy of self-annihilation, the same pull that drew MacDonald and Wallace, Chesnutt and Smith.

Just so low, so heartbroken. Can't even properly cry and release it; willing myself to sob but the tears won't flow; looking in the bathroom cabinet to see what I could kill myself with. No hope of anything now. How tempting just to end everything, to stop struggling. Is suicide cowardly? Isn't that just the propaganda of the living?

Only when I began to own – to incorporate – the 'hated, humiliated' part of myself did the fantasies of suicide abate. For the fantasy is really that we can rid ourselves of that part and then be reborn as enviable and desirable. As Schopenhauer wrote, 'suicide is the supreme assertion of the will, and at the opposite pole from the renunciation that could alone give release'. Based on what he wrote, I must conclude that Ian MacDonald would have agreed with that great philosopher of pessimism. But in his darkest hour he remained at war with himself, and alone in that war.

● ● ●

Did man invent God to replace the Father who wasn't there – our protector, our absent champion? In a world of chaotic violence, most of it caused by frightened and frightening men, is 'God' just an abstracted version of what we'd like a patriarch to be? Perhaps all religion is simply a metaphor for what's missing.

If our parents are the only gods we know as we grow through pre-verbal infancy into childhood, what happens to our budding personal theology when those gods don't protect us but instead neglect or hurt us? What picture of the cosmos do we then assemble in our minds? More than anything we need the unconditional embrace of Donald Winnicott's 'good-enough' mother, whose presence we take for granted and from whose enclosing arms we slowly move out into the world.

Jean Liedloff, formulator of the 'continuum concept' – the notion that babies should be carried by their parents for as long as possible – believed addiction (particularly to opiates) was one of the most direct 'expressions of in-arms deprivation' and suggested that '[the addict] cannot resist returning, guiltily, hounded, ragged and sick, to what in fact was his birthright to experience'.

If my own indoctrinated conditioning resisted Liedloff's belief that the addict's incompleteness and 'disease' derive from a radical lack of 'in-arms' experience as an infant, I knew in my heart that I'd repeatedly returned to heroin in the way she was describing. I'd gone back to it because it held me, cocooned me; because it loved me in a way nothing else had loved me. For the deprived infant, Liedloff wrote, 'Self is wanting, waiting; Other is withholding, unresponsive or opposing.' Heroin never withheld from me, and only opposed me when I couldn't obtain it.

My own parents were typical of a war-traumatized generation of young mothers and fathers who themselves had had little 'in-arms' experience, legatees of the stern Victorian belief that children should not be heard, barely be seen and certainly not be held. (My maternal uncle once confessed to me that he'd never once been hugged by his mother in his life.) Though they responded warmly to physical embrace in their eighties, my mother and father were as physically affectionate as most of their contemporaries – which is to say, not very – and didn't have a surplus of the stuff to pass on.

My father, who as a twelve-year-old had lost his own father during the 1940 defence of Calais, boasted of his ability to put emotions in what he called 'deep freeze'. My mother, meanwhile, suffered post-natal depression and found it hard to comfort a distressed son. Her husband came home from work to hear his son screaming in a cot while she sat catatonically in the kitchen. When on another occasion Lotta – the Swedish au pair who may have been the prototype 'love of my life' – went to pick me up as I cried, my mother told her not to be 'so silly'.

I understand these reactions and to an extent inherited them. When my own infant sons screamed, I could hardly bear it and wanted to punish them for the agony they caused me.

Jake has been screaming almost nonstop this evening, and I am not sure I can stand another second of it. In fact, I'm not sure I am capable of feeling any pity or even real love for this bundle of skin and bone who only demands and screams and shows no more acknowledgement of one's presence than that. When he cries unremittingly I feel like my heart is going to burst, and I want only to punish him for the distress he is causing me. My wife cries out of compassion for his suffering; I just want to die because I cannot bear the noise.

Fortunately I knew the poor mites were not deliberately persecuting me; knew too that holding and comforting them only made things better. What I wanted, above all, was to give them the security and self-assurance I lacked – to know, without having to question it, that they were loved for no other reason than that they were alive. 'Freedom will only come when I believe I deserve joy simply because I exist,' Antony said to me thirty years after we'd last used drugs together, 'rather than because I think I've earned it through being dutiful.'

Sometimes I cannot believe I have a son, that I am his protector, when most of the time I am myself such a wide-eyed child. The question 'Do I feel safe enough in the world for both of us?' popped into my mind today.

It may be that addiction is inherently narcissistic, or at least symptomatic of a narcissistic response to neglect. Invariably it involves a process of feeding – or *glutting* – the self because one was not 'fed' as one should have been as a child. Distrusting the proffered love of others, the narcissistic child remains within a fantasy world he can control. As Thomas Moore asked in his *Care of the Soul*, 'Is our negative branding of narcissism a defense against a demanding call of the soul to be loved?' Only a sincere desire to emerge from the prison of my own making brings me into the world of others.

To be loved – 'to call myself beloved, to feel myself beloved on the earth', in Raymond Carver's sublime phrase – is surely all any of us really wants or needs; that, and to love in return. But if we lack the in-arms experience of love at our core, we can't conjure it out of thin air. Furthermore, I'm all too conscious that mere in-arms deprivation would have been a result for the countless addicts who were beaten, raped, and otherwise psychologically annihilated as kids. I've heard stories that made me wonder how their narrators were still alive, how they carried their memories of abuse and continued to function at all. We now know how children become so inured to abuse that they develop an outer shell no therapist can pierce. At best these kids become sociopathic; at worst, *psycho*pathic. Both are extreme forms of narcissism that make empathy unimaginable.

'You cannot underestimate the suicidality of these kids,' says Camilla Batmanghelidjh, who'd be the first to say one should never give up on any child, no matter how contemptuous s/he is of the love being offered. I once heard a girl talk of a teacher who – in a school where she'd otherwise known only shame and persecution – had ruffled her hair and smiled at her. She said the gesture, as innocuous as it was, may have saved her life. And it made me think this: *Reach out and touch someone. Take that risk. You cannot know the difference it might make.*

How, if I hate myself – or, at least, continuously split off the 'hated, humiliated' part of me – do I heal and become whole? Is it possible for those who weren't comforted as kids to achieve self-acceptance, to love themselves as they love the dearest people in their life? Will they not always feel the wound at their core? (A certain aloneness and alienation is clearly endemic to our existence, yet there are people whose unconscious memory of 'in-arms' love affords them a sense of what Aldous Huxley called 'the world's fundamental All-Rightness in spite of pain, death and bereavement'.)

In the early months of my recovery I heard people say, 'You're right where you're supposed to be.' And I took comfort in that notion, since it briefly assuaged the fear that I was doing something wrong – or should have been doing *something else, with other people, in a different place.* Yet, left to myself for any length of time, I soon reverted to the dread that right here was precisely where I should not be: *I was missing out, missing the point.* 'One lives so badly,' said Rilke, 'because one always comes into the present unfinished, unable, distracted.' I could not see that I remained so ashamed, so sure that at root I was unlovable and destined to be alone.

Self-obsession, it transpired, was nothing more than the obsessive search for a self that could integrate with the world, that had a place and could rub along with other selves: *I'm okay, you're okay.* Most of the time I could not have expressed the equation in those terms. Even after I came to terms with elements of myself I didn't like – and made a concerted effort to believe I was not inherently bad – I was left with the underlying fear that others saw through my surface to the repulsive core within.

Nowhere was this more evident than in dealings with women, whose ascribed power to reject and abandon was almost too much to bear. Convinced my desire would deter any girl I liked, more often than not I avoided the risk of exposing her to it at all. Meanwhile I was speechless with admiration for any friend who – without the aid of drugs – could make a play for a pretty woman. If I ended up in bed with a girl, usually it was she who'd been the seducer.

Love comes in many guises. The approval of my peers in work was loaded with the same expectation and dependency, the writer's always-fragile ego permanently at the mercy of editors who – with a single unreturned phone call or a criticism – had the power to crush me. When you have no innate conviction that you're okay or even possess some talent, it requires so little to pull the rug from under you. It took me twenty-five years to believe that my own opinion of my work – even if I was wrong about it – was more important than anyone else's. But then it took me twenty-five years to grasp that if I like myself, others' dislike of me is all but irrelevant.

• • •

What really completed the process of healing – to the extent that it's ever completed – was something wholly unexpected. It began with a rift, a year of not speaking to my parents, triggered by the silliest of things: the shame I felt as I heard them whispering crossly about my youngest son marching through their house with muddy boots. Something in me erupted in that instant, and I returned to London to try to make sense of it. Talking regularly with my sister, who'd always been the family's go-to black sheep, I went back to feelings I'd buried since childhood – or, rather, *in* childhood – and allowed them to rise to the surface.

I steeped myself in books by Alice Miller, from her ground-breaking *Drama of Being a Child* to the formidable *For Your Own Good*. 'We cannot require parents to face something they are unable to face,' Miller had uncompromisingly written, 'but we can keep confronting them with the knowledge that it was not suffering *per se* that made their child ill but its repression, which was essential for the sake of the parents.'

For all the years I'd spent in recovery and therapy, I had never directly accessed the suffering I'd buried – or the suffering of the burial itself, the shame of having and showing feelings. Moreover, it only now dawned on me that I hadn't properly separated from my parents because I continued to seek their approval. The psychic umbilical cord had never been properly cut. I had not rebelled as I should have, only acted out the rebellion.

'What if, instead of "reframing" my emotions, I simply welcomed them and allowed them to be *fully felt*,' Brandon Bays wrote in *The Journey*, a New-Agey volume I would ordinarily have scorned but which now assisted me in dropping back into excruciating moments from childhood as though I were once again a skinny, shivering boy. To embrace that unheard stripling, to clasp him to my adult self and commit to protecting him, was now imperative. I knew I'd been running away from him all my adult life, and that all my depressions and anxieties were rooted in his shame and neglect.

Trying always to stay one step ahead of one's pain: this is the root cause of all anxiety.

Could it be that, as Philip Larkin famously described it, emotional illness involved little more than man's handing on misery from generation to generation? Was it that simple? And what chance did I or anyone else have to break that cycle? How could I find enough love for myself to pass it on to my kids?

Pietro Citati says Kafka longed for the joy of having children while knowing he never would. 'He imagined that only by having children can we forget our ego, dissolve "the anguish of the nerves" . . . abandon ourselves to that passive quietude and tender relaxation which the continuity of generations assures.' Alas, Citati was only half-right: some of us still long to be Kafka . . .

To this day, almost fifteen years later, I'm certain that taking my 'Journey' – with a kind woman on a cosy houseboat near Hampton Court as sunlight streamed through her windows – profoundly changed me, or at least changed the relationship between my Self and the universe. I'd gone armed with forty years' worth of scepticism and yet was willing to release the pain that had fuelled my addictive avoidance.

Trusting the woman on her houseboat, I closed my eyes and surrendered to her guidance, descending through layers of self-protection to what I can only frame as an apprehension of infinite love – the part of me that's beyond loss. The Journey was as close as I've come to a palpable intuition of God, to knowing I'm a part of the whole and loved merely because I exist.

Invited to voice what I'd always longed to say to my parents, I raged and wept and let it all go. And the legacy of that release is with me today. I became a free man as a result of it, able to see my mother and father as simply two more of God's children rather than as deities I needed either to please or to reject. I emerged from the shadow of my father's power to stand before him as a man in my own right, to hold to my own values and principles without having to comply with or impress him. I didn't need to slay the *pater*, simply to make peace with myself. I loved him, admired him, disagreed with him.

Perhaps what I underwent on the houseboat was a kind of primal therapy, facing and reliving the original pain of abandonment in order to free myself of my desperate dependency. Perhaps we all have to face that abandonment before we can begin a relationship with the larger world.

● ● ●

It's been said that the depressed person would rather be good than be happy. Until the breakthrough on the houseboat, depression was a frequent feature of my life. Therapy helped staunch its self-destructive power but never quite dissolved it. If depression is internalized rage rooted in what Liedloff termed 'the wrongness of self', it follows that depression cannot lift until the self becomes 'right'. When the fundament of my being is structurally unsound, depression always resurfaces, triggered by the most innocuous events.

For years my belief was that I was different from and less than others. Unless I was on some artificial high caused by drugs – or, in recovery, by a mood-altering change in my fortunes – simply walking down a London street could make me feel 'wrong'.

No one sees me. I search people's eyes for signs of kinship but there's nothing. I'm invisible. The best I can do is stay manically busy with work, on the basis that stress is preferable to depression. But then comes night, when there's nothing to obscure the nothingness of my existence. I'm in the pits of aloneness, at the core of my loveless inner child. All is lack. I can't even call people for fear of having this confirmed.

Is there a paradox in the very notion of self-esteem? Could it not be said that the surer a person's sense of Self, the smaller the size of that person's ego will be? In *The House of Mirth*, Edith Wharton wrote of Lily Bart's 'feeling of being something rootless and ephemeral, mere spindrift of the whirling surface of existence, without anything to which the poor little tentacles of self could cling before the awful flood submerged them'. As I examine that dizzying sentence I think: another person might feel quite happy being mere spindrift, but only because the core of her being was sure and unjeopardized.

But then what does it mean to 'know thyself'? What *is* this Self? Is it just a model for an epiphenomenon whose role is to simplify complex reality, a frame the mind creates to burrow its way through overwhelming otherness? While I crave a narrative that makes sense of the random happenstance of my life – a *self-narration* that memorializes and redeems it – the language-driven engagement with narrative is precisely what drives my exhausting egomania. 'Every ego is schizophrenic,' Eckhart Tolle wrote in *A New Earth*; 'the notion of "my life" is the original delusion of separateness and the source of ego.'

Regarded from another standpoint, the Self is the by-product of raw instinct: *I must survive*. The three primary drives – for security, status, sexual love – are what produce the phantasm of ego, and anything that threatens them provokes resentment. The better fed and more prosperous I am, the more spurious my private self becomes. Far from being simply the universal 'I' that sees and hears and touches – the nexus in which the flux of life coheres – Self becomes a monumentalized noun and source of anxious comparison, obsessed with others in a symmetrical rather than complementary way.

While capitalism persuades me that my Self matters terribly, secretly I long to meld with the universe and abandon the ego that insists on difference. Collective joy – the Dionysian ecstasy espoused by Nietzsche – gives me explosive release from the angst and inadequacy of the bourgeois self. 'I have such a feeling of solidarity with everything alive,' Einstein wrote in 1944, 'that it doesn't seem to me important where the individual ends or begins.' This is also what quantum physics tells me: that I'm part of the *is-ness*, Buber's 'streaming mutual life of the universe', Simone Weil's 'chain of mutual compensations of energy'. String theory, suggesting the building blocks of the universe are not blocks at all but tiny vibrating loops, may prove to be the purest refutation yet of the idea that anything – least of all the Self – is fixed in time and space as a distinct entity. If everything I see or hear or touch is the same ceaseless energy of Nowness, why do I strive so hard to assert superiority, inferiority, difference? Why do I take my life so personally?

I have a choice: I can, if I really wish to drop out of the rat race to nowhere, forgo the need to win and to prove myself – to matter to others rather than to give to them. But it's not a freedom earned by learning, and certainly not by reading a book. Freedom comes only from a moment of revelation, an intuition that all my restless questing – for comfort, respect, status, happiness, meaning itself – is a delusion.

The Poor Little Tentacles Of Self

The great question that life poses each day is surely this: *Can I be happy even if I don't get what I want?*

• • •

Extending myself to others is always an existential effort and always costs something. Which is why it means so much when I do it. Innately selfish because I believe I need to be, I don't want to stop thinking about my own needs or start thinking about yours. *I'll get to you in a minute – right now I have to finish THIS, which is so much more important than YOU. I'm an unfinished work in progress that must attain its goal to achieve completion. If you force me to break off from what I'm doing – to deviate from the monomaniacal track I am on – then I will be incomplete, fragmented, broken. Let me reach my destination and I'll be ALL YOURS.*

Even when we talk, I will interrupt you because I need to be heard more than I need to hear. I'll try to fix your messy, unruly pain with a few quick aphorisms rather than let you get it all out. But if I can just be still and silent and resist the compulsion to play God – to accept that I may not have any answers and may not even understand what you are saying – then a minor miracle occurs. You might hear yourself in your talking and perhaps answer your own questions. I need only be present.

Moving from loveless self-aggrandizement to quiet empathy is a journey that takes forever – or a nanosecond.

It begins with compassion for myself, and with the integration of the fragments that make up my consciousness. Then I can get out of my own way.

Imagine not being fixated on *one thing* and instead being aware of the life bubbling beneath what Marion Milner called the 'deliberate surface of consciousness' – to be alive to all that happens around me, with a broad rather than narrow attention. The more I free myself of the grooves of my routines, and the more I treat my supposed sense of purpose with a smiling scepticism, the richer my life becomes.

If the neoliberal materialism that brought about the collapse of the global financial system is actually a kind of idolatrous religion, then what the world needs now is a kind of *immaterialism* – a simple awareness that we can't trap happiness in a jar. Our boom-and-bust cycles will continue, for greed will always outstrip satisfaction, but perhaps these times will bring about a new notion of Enough.

● ● ●

In Kevin Avery's *Everything is an Afterthought*, his biography-cum-anthology of the great rock writer Paul Nelson, an irresistible moment occurs when *Rolling Stone* founder-editor Jann Wenner strides into Nelson's office to announce the magazine will henceforth operate a star-ratings policy for its record reviews. The story goes that Nelson marched out of the office, never to return.

'That,' said his fellow *Stone* contributor Dave Marsh, 'is the death of rock criticism right there.'

Why is it we no longer have the time to digest an album or book or film review without the advance steer of a star (or marks-out-of-five) rating? Why are we in such a hurry to get past the verbiage to the decision to buy or not to buy? Is it because we're all so hopelessly addicted to *the next big thing*? And is the World Wide Web a symptom or a cause of that addiction? Or both?

'Rather than public ritual,' Evan Eisenberg could write as early as 1996, 'what the World Wide Web seems to encourage is private ritual of an especially nervous, addictive kind.' Nowhere is such addiction more evident than in the social media that barely existed when Eisenberg was writing. At the tap of a screen I'm an *instant orator*, egged on to have my uncontained say on matters I've barely thought about. What does the compulsion to post and tweet – on anything and everything – say about a culture in which ostensible omni-connectedness masks the increasing atomization of society? I'm in thrall to my phone or laptop or tablet, barely able to raise my eyes to make the most fleeting human connection. Step away from Facebook or Twitter for ten seconds and it's clear I'm not much more than a cog in a virtual machine, my words mere means for corporations to market to me and my 'friends'.

My narcissistic confessions and hubristic rapid-fire opinions are the fuel on which social media rely. Once upon a time we were connected to a few people we really knew and who really knew *us*. We felt community with our family and friends, and only the written word extended the world beyond that community. Then came radio and television, bringing that world into our homes with a pseudo intimacy and immediacy. McLuhan was right: the medium had become its own message.

Now, forty years since I first watched a colour TV as a boy, I'm relentlessly connected to an influx of information – accurate or otherwise – about what's happening beyond my purview. It's literally *more than I can take*, unless I consciously elect to unplug from the grid. Every blipping noise urges me to chase the elusive connection I no longer feel in my soul. *I'm connected, therefore I am.*

This contraction of attention further foments the appetite for rapid judgement and tabloid condemnation, making trolls of us all. I no longer have time to experience my fellow humans as kindred suffering spirits. 'There is at present a dearth of humane imagination for the integrity and mystery of other lives,' Marilynne Robinson wrote. 'In consequence, the nimbus of art and learning and reflection that has dignified our troubled presence on this planet seems now like a thinning atmosphere.'

Even unplugging from the grid can't rewrite the fact that technology has irreversibly altered me, perhaps even changed the molecular structure of my brain. For my children this may not be a problem – they seem to multi-task without perceptible anxiety – but for those who've lived through the traumatic changes of the last three decades there's a desperate nostalgia for a time when we had fewer choices, when we were *present in our play* and not ceaselessly displaced by networks of pseudo-community. The teenagers I see standing together on street corners with their smartphones don't look anxious or fretful: it's the norm for them not to be fully present in that space and moment. Perhaps their gadgets are benignly extending them into 'the larger world' and I should learn to stop worrying.

If the new technologies push me to chase a fulfilment that's forever out of reach, it's because I've been beguiled into believing happiness really *is* around the corner. In the words of writer George Saunders, 'it feels like I've re-programmed myself to become discontent with whatever I'm doing faster'. As it's always done, advertising abets addiction by convincing me I'm incomplete and need to be made whole. Mounted on the back of envy, aspiration strains to reach the summit, only to find a more dwarfing peak when it arrives there.

'Happiness', now measured by government-endorsed indices, has become a birthright rather than an incidental and intermittent by-product. I stamp my feet when I don't get my way. For Nietzsche, to regard pain as 'a defect of existence' – as an evil, even – resulted from subscribing to a 'religion of comfortableness'. But it may be more even than that: a regression, in fact, to an infantile refusal not to have my needs met *now*. Chasing happiness – especially in the form of pleasure – may be the surest guarantor of misery on earth.

• • •

I should declare the deeper paradox of writing these words at all. For if the spiritual life turns out not to be a search for meaning but a release from it, then do I perhaps defeat myself in the very effort to articulate the small revelations I've been granted as a recovering addict? 'What could I say to you that would be of value,' Siddhartha tells Govinda in Hesse's famous novel, 'except that perhaps you seek too much, that as a result of your seeking you cannot find.'

Perhaps all my ordered life is just a neurotic disorder, a futile effort to repress the 'base desires' in me. Updike describes writing itself as 'an addiction, an illusory release, a presumptuous taming of reality'. And yet one must live by Apollonian constraint or destroy oneself. Is that life's greatest joke? I realize that most of what I do involves imposing form on formless emotion. It's the formlessness of my inner life I find so difficult. Through art one strives to lock life into place.

I'm also keenly aware that simply by ageing one becomes, to a degree, more comfortable with oneself, less ridden by angst. Perhaps I learned nothing at all from my suffering but simply lost the brain cells that caused me such grief. As Proust wrote, with an exquisite sigh, 'everything comes about just as we desired it, but only when we no longer desire it'. Yet if all art is born of the same need to fix or even stop the world – to frame or contain its chaos – is it not also art that stills the flux of time and space for long enough to see the world as it is?

Even as I suspect that death renders it futile, I long to believe my life means something. While the Buddhist accepts his ego is a droplet falling into an infinite ocean, I remain haunted by death, desperate to leave behind a mark of my existence. In my twenties I didn't really believe I would die; even in my thirties death remained remote and unreal. Only in my forties did the first intimations of mortality really seep into my soul. And then, in the following decade, even as I turned and flinched from it, I actively entertained the prospect of my ending. I awoke with inexplicable palpitations in the night, terrified the end might be moments away. I sighed as I realized a still-fresh memory of joy or pain referenced an event that occurred a decade ago – that time was ushering me ever faster towards oblivion.

I try not to hate myself for getting older. I'm not getting older because of something I've done wrong; I believe it's better to fade away than to burn out. Yet life is now shot through with Ending, striated by it to the point where death-awareness almost incapacitates me and makes me wonder why I bother with chores and checklists. Nothing prepares us for the pathos or poignancy of this age, when we're already losing dear friends to fatal diseases. Though we made scant effort to see them while they were alive, the thought of not seeing them again is almost unbearable. Inane as it is to give voice to the melancholy of late middle age – to grief, to regret over losses great and small – it's hard not to wail silently, to feel bewildered by the quickening of time.

The denial or sublimation of the fear of dying accounts for much misery. I tell myself I accept my death, that an anxious clinging to life is no way to live, but it isn't really true. Reason tells me I will just end, but fear says death may be the beginning of an unknown, a crossing into darkness and aloneness or worse: the Hell of the world's collective nightmares. It should be consolation that death is where we're all headed, yet the passing is framed as the most solitary of exits, an expulsion from the world. Thank God, I think, that I don't have to go just yet.

When my friend Jo was dying of cancer, I longed to ask if she was afraid. But right to the end she thought she'd survive and not die, even when she lay curled in bed, hairless as a baby but with even less flesh on her bones, smiling sweetly as she reported the doctors were pleased with her white-cell count . . . or with *something*. I couldn't even take it in, so heartbroken was I to see her lying there.

It's so wrong that she's gone, so touching that just a week ago she still thought she would make it, a little bald child curled up with her cat and the morphine kicking in. I'm always shocked that a person can just be gone, that you'll never hear her voice again other than as a recording in your head. And I'm guilty that I'm alive, without cancer, with hopes and dreams, wondering why she needed to suffer so much. She was unique and beautiful, wild and fiercely honest, brave and strangely naïve. What a mystery that she no longer exists . . .

How would I feel if a doctor informed me I had three months to live? The thought makes me reel. Yet I'm also prepared for the bad news at all hours. Like many, I suppose, I wonder what I'd do on receiving a death sentence. Begin a futile battle against it? Plan a tour of the world's wonders? Or just lie in soothingly hot baths reading cancer memoirs?

Jo regularly pops into my mind, often to admonish me for being so gloomy when I still draw breath. Guilt follows as I remember what a eulogist would no doubt call her 'insatiable appetite for life'. What she'd have given for six more months of swimming and cycling and yoga retreats, whereas here am I with myriad choices and opportunities, asking myself what is 'the point of it all'. She'd say that the point is just to be present for whatever happens – to be alert and alive to experience – and to give as you'd be given to.

There are consolations. Many of those who've known it is fast approaching have grasped that death is precisely what makes life matter. On the day he was diagnosed with inoperable pancreatic cancer and given ten months to live, guitarist Wilko Johnson recalled that he 'walked outside into a beautiful winter's day and felt this rush of elation. I was alive! Alive!' For playwright Dennis Potter, nearing his end in 1994, the 'nowness of everything' was 'absolutely wondrous'. For Apple's Steve Jobs, 'all external expectations – all pride, all fear of embarrassment or failure' fell away in the face of death. To accept it – *pace* Dylan Thomas, *not* to rage against the dying of the light – was for him the ultimate freedom.

None of us can say with certainty there's no afterlife, but to the rational agnostic mind it's a consoling fantasy based on the unbearable idea of not living or worse: the horror of an endless void. If instead I could live as though time itself were beautiful and not frightening, I would surely be in paradise, flowing through the nowness of everything, each moment the same moment. Even the words 'now' and 'moment' are vain efforts to pause time, to deny that we're moving in it and that it will take away everything we try to hold on to. Such is surely the point of meditation: not to enforce stillness but to flow with the universe's ceaseless change.

Where Eastern religions are based on assumptions of relativity and of interconnection with all life, Western man insatiably alienates himself, objectifying his ego rather than simply being his feelings. To have or to be, noun or verb; that's the choice. I am not a monument to be venerated but, rather, a fluid and fluctuating event that passes into the ether. Which is why graveyards symbolize denial, every burial plot a futile clinging to life: we can't let our loved ones go because we're so frightened of going ourselves. But then every photograph I take – and paste into an album – is a similar clinging to something that's already gone.

A day of deep dread. As Bateson makes clear in Angels Fear, *I'm driven mad by illusory attachments. Having done no tangible work this week, I feel lost, confused, fuzzy-headed. What does it mean to say 'I don't like myself'? What is this 'my-self' from which I split away? Is it only the approximate idea of how others see me, haunting me as I fight to maintain the delusion of separate identity?*

It was Bateson who saw that the Twelve Steps of Alcoholics Anonymous proposed a complementary Eastern solution to the torturous paradox of the self-hating egomaniac – the *ism* of Western alcoholism. As Harry M. Tiebout noted in his 1944 essay 'The Therapeutic Mechanism of AA', 'the patient . . . shows he has become aware of the fact that, *as he ceases the effort to maintain his individuality* [my italics], he can relax and enjoy life in a quiet yet thoroughly satisfying way'. To any recovering addict striving to prove himself – to arrive at a place where others will value and honour him – I say only this: *You're already there, you just can't see it yet.*

But how do I come to the belief that everything's already okay; that despite making plans and decisions in anticipation of a future that never arrives, I only torment myself through the futile effort to secure happiness? Forced to live with the vertiginous dread that demands of me what I wish to do next, if I surrender to the flow of life and do 'the next right thing' as I intuitively sense it as a choice, the angst of decision-making ceases. When my eyes and ears are open, the universe tells me what to do and what to accept. I'm right where I'm supposed to be.

● ● ●

I am not my work. I'm not my family. I'm not my marriage. I'm not my home. I'm not my salary. I'm not my car. I'm not my clothes. I'm not my achievements. I am *this*. I am the cosmos. I am you. There's a deeper Self that moves beyond Ego and its attachments – what David Lynch calls 'the self of all that is'.

I crave to be confirmed, to be shown almost continuously that my existence makes a difference. If I'm not having an effect on someone or everyone, then I do not exist. As William Hazlitt wrote in his 1821 essay 'On Living to One's Self', 'infinite are the mortifications of the bare attempt to emerge from obscurity . . .'

True freedom stems from not caring what others think of me. Freeing myself of dependent attachments (to people, places, objects, beliefs, habits), I connect to a vertical sense of self that isn't time-bound but is eternally now and eternally right. In the groups I attend I regularly hear people talk about 'getting a better perspective on our lives'. The best perspective of all might be a view from outer space.

At the root of my thirst to make life mean something – to others and thus to myself – is an aching desire for a unity I'll never attain. For the scientific historian George Sarton, people can broadly be divided into 'those who suffer the tormenting desire for unity and those who do not'. Between the two, he said, lies an abyss: 'The "unitary" is the troubled; the other is the peaceful.' Those who crave unity are the ones who feel radically unattached and unconsciously long to return to the womb. Those who detach – who accept life as, in Richard Ford's words, 'teeming and befuddling' – are paradoxically those who feel most grounded in the world.

Sometimes humour is all I have to help me stay sane. But if I must take myself seriously, I must also accept my absurdity. No one's saying we shouldn't take suffering seriously, just that people generally suffer because *others* take life too seriously. The key is to *know eternity*, as the *Tao Te Ching* counsels – to see that nothing is forever, least of all our selves. The terrible, entirely liberating truth is that I'm expendable: '*Life goes on without me.*'

If the only security lies in accepting life's many insecurities, then freedom flows solely from accepting my irrelevance in the face of change and death. When I learn the art of dying – dying to myself before my physical death – I begin to live.

• • •

I wish I could say that I've implemented these life lessons. On some days there's peace, acceptance, love. On rather more days I'm powerless to arrest the anxious, wounded, controlling, void-stuffing need in me – the restless rush to catch something that forever slips my grasp. I'm afraid of losing what I have and scared I won't get what I want. And usually I can trace it all back to the unshakable conviction that I *matter*.

Addiction manifests in my life principally in the restless sense that I need more (love, money, respect, status) and that enough is not Enough. Life then gets too much and stress sinks me. I panic that the water is rising over my mouth and nostrils.

Decompressing after two days of hyperventilating stress. How can I still experience the same terrifying anxiety I felt 27 years ago, when I first stopped self-medicating? Is there no hope of lasting peace of mind? The bare facts are that I experience dwindling cash reserves as walls closing in; that I lack all perspective when it comes to money; that I feel hopeless and helpless; that tension mounts in my body to a level close to intolerable; and that I feel paralysing shame at my inability to make ends meet.

When my friend Paul talks of 'the addiction to busyness', I plead guilty as charged. It's easy to rationalize the frantic paddling under the surface as responsibility. On the good days I say, 'I've got this far and haven't been left stranded.' On the bad ones I think, 'What if I don't get my slice of the pie?'

I don't sleep so well. I get grouchy and snappy. I bite my nails and chew my cuticles. I'm like most people I know, caught up in capitalism's race to nowhere. I expect more of the world than it can ever give me. I try too hard to prove (or improve) myself. I need to fail better. I don't know how to reconcile the practical business of breadwinning – or, worse, delusional empire-building – with the deepening awareness that it's all a beautiful joke. Apocalyptic floods could wash it all away tomorrow. They *do* and I daily numb myself to others' devastations.

If I really stop and breathe deeply in meditation – which I started properly only in 2014 – I detach better from the ego's demands. I'm not there yet, but I'm clean and connected in ways I never thought possible. Much of the time there's joy and laughter, the incidental bliss of noticing the world and other people. One might almost call this grace, even a return to innocence: what Henry James described as 'the wordless fact itself . . . the uncontested possession of the long sweet stupid day'. Left to my own limited devices, I *will* revert to avoidance, denial, self-annihilation. If enough is not Enough, More will never suffice.

I keep showing up. The healing goes on.

Surrender

On this day, as on other days, let me let go
the desperate clinging will.
Deliver me from heroin and lead me not into crack dens.
Help me forgo self-centred fear
and all that issues from the pit of dread that says
I haven't what I need and won't get what I want:
the greed and envious lack,
self-pity and self-loathing, thrusting lust,
procrastination of the next right thing,
resentment, expectation –
take it all.

Let me accept this life entirely as it stands,
change only what I can and what requires the change,
and let me live in thankfulness
for every large and paltry thing that's come my way:
the roof over the head, the fullness in the gut
and all of the immeasurables
of love and friendship, kindness, care.
On this day, as on other days, let me extend myself to all
and move beyond the lonesome soul.

Acknowledgements

My great thanks to: Andreas Campomar, Claire Chesser, Linda Silverman, Jess Gulliver, Matthew Hamilton, and Jonny Geller. To my sister Tam, to Paul Sunderland and of course to Christian. To my sons Jake, Fred and Nat, and to my stepsons George and Fred. Of course to my beloved wife Natalie, whose support has been unwavering. And to all who've trudged the happy road with me.